HOW TO ENJOY
ARCHITECTURE

A House for Essex by FAT and Grayson Perry.

HOW TO ENJOY
ARCHITECTURE

A Guide for Everyone

CHARLES HOLLAND

YALE UNIVERSITY PRESS
New Haven and London

For information about this and other Yale University Press publications, please contact:
U.S. Office: sales.press@yale.edu   yalebooks.com
Europe Office: sales@yaleup.co.uk   yalebooks.co.uk

Set in Garamond by Tetragon, London
Printed in Slovenia by DZS-Grafik d.o.o.

Library of Congress Control Number: 2023952217

ISBN 978-0-300-26393-0

A catalogue record for this book is available from the British Library.

10 9 8 7 6 5 4 3 2 1

For my mother, Frances Gillian

CONTENTS

FIGURES

INTRODUCTION

How can we enjoy architecture? Architecture is useful – essential, even. It is profoundly bound up with how we live, how we organise ourselves and how these things have evolved historically. We know too that sometimes architecture aspires to the status of art. Important and vital things, but none of them necessarily about enjoyment.

This book could have been called *How to Read Architecture* or even *How to Understand Architecture*. But neither of those titles would have captured a sense of the pleasure in looking at and experiencing buildings. They sound worthy and important and quite probably highly stimulating. But enjoyable? Well, it depends where one finds enjoyment. This book is not an excuse for being incurious or less knowledgeable. But it *is* grounded in an experience of looking at buildings and predicated on trying to share some of the joy of that experience.

Enjoyment is a key part of how I experience architecture. When I design, there is a profound enjoyment in the process, in the challenge and the satisfaction of resolving that challenge. But I go looking for architecture too, loving the thrill of tracking down buildings I have always wanted to see. Sometimes I stumble across it and I keep an eye out for things I find stimulating or surprising. I have learnt to look at architecture, and this book is partly about trying to share what I have found. Of course, architecture also tells me a lot of things about people and places and the history of both. But looking at, experiencing, *using* architecture can bring enjoyment in itself, and it is this that I have tried to write about.

So what tools and skills can we use to better understand and appreciate the buildings that surround us? For most of us, architecture is experienced in a daze of habit: the rooms of our own home, a building spotted from the top of the bus that means that it's time to get off, a familiar landmark on a routine car journey. Architecture intersects with our daily lives in ways that are immediate but also mundane, and for much of the time we push it to the back of our minds. We see it, we orient ourselves by it, but we don't always really *look* at it. Or if we do, it might only be to pass negative judgements about a new housing development where we live, or a modern public building that we find hard to like.

Yet this day-to-day familiarity is also one of the things that is so interesting about architecture. Buildings shape our lives in ways that are both subtle and obvious. We meet people in architecture. We are educated in it, get married in it, fall in and out of love in it, have children, grow up, go to school, work, eat, sleep and live in it. Buildings bring us together, separate us, shape our days and host our nights out.

Architecture frames our lives. We constantly move between buildings and rooms. We follow their codes of behaviour, whether it's the quiet contemplation of an art gallery or the raucousness of a bar on a Friday night. Architecture can also be highly divisive. Buildings occasionally cause controversy, and we can have strong feelings about them. Sometimes we object to them being built when they inconvenience us or replace something we care about. We campaign to save them when they are threatened with demolition or redevelopment. We may object to them because we consider them inappropriate or feel that they represent values we don't care for.

Sometimes it feels as if architecture is done *to* us, an imposition brought about by powerful, unaccountable forces. Anyone who has taken part in a public consultation on architecture knows how strong emotions are when it comes to new buildings or proposed developments. Architecture affects our environment profoundly and it mostly happens without our explicit approval.

On the other hand, buildings also engage us. We visit them at weekends for pleasure. Sometimes we even go on holiday to see them. They draw tourists and are fawned over in coffee-table books and travel guides. TV programmes, magazines and the apps on our phones are full of houses and homes and interior makeovers. Architecture is both popular and oddly enigmatic, a subject that interests us intensely but that we ignore for much of the time, too. This book aims to help us notice, understand and enjoy the buildings around us. It will help develop skills and tools that will open a door to the stories behind buildings, the decisions that have shaped them and the histories they embody. But more importantly, it aims to help us to enjoy buildings more and alert us to the pleasures of architecture.

How to Enjoy Architecture

This is a book about architecture, how to look at it, experience it and enjoy it. It is about the visual pleasure of buildings. It is about the materials they are made of and the way these materials are composed and brought together into compositions and patterns and arrangements. It is about how buildings work together to make bits of a city or streets or villages. It is about variety and how buildings relate to each other, about visual harmony and how sometimes visual disharmony is a good thing. It is about looking: about learning how to look and what to look for.

In her 1964 essay 'Against Interpretation', the American writer Susan Sontag argued that there is a bias in art criticism towards the literary over the visual. Sontag suggested that there is a critical assumption that meaning is something that lies *behind* works of art, hidden and hard, perhaps impossible, to see. The meaning of a painting, for instance, is something that needs to be interpreted in order to reveal the truth of what we are looking at. In this sense, the qualities of a work of art (or architecture) that we can see or touch are considered less reliable than things that aren't, such as the historical context in which it was made or the intentions of the artist when they made it.

For this reason, the language of art criticism sometimes encourages us to ignore the object in front of us. Regular visitors to art galleries will be familiar with the lengthy captions telling us what a particular painting or sculpture means, what it is about and what the painter or sculptor wanted to express. These notices are helpful and well intentioned but they also have the effect of taking our attention away from what we came to look at. They suggest not only that there is a single meaning to discover but also that we can discover this meaning not by looking at the work but by reading a caption instead.

Sontag went on to say that 'what is needed is a vocabulary – a descriptive, rather than prescriptive, vocabulary – for forms'. This book is written partly in response to that plea. It is intended to help provide such a vocabulary, in this case for buildings and works of architecture. Art and architecture are discursive subjects: that is, they are part of wider intellectual and ideological frameworks. They don't exist in a vacuum. I don't mean to deny the importance of critical and theoretical writings about art. But I agree with Sontag's assertion that we tend to believe meaning when it is written down more than when it is painted, sculpted or built. This book is written in the conviction that works of art are not necessarily vessels carrying meaning from elsewhere but are ideas in *themselves*.

Sontag was writing about works of art, not architecture. You might argue that very different conditions apply. Buildings are not removed from the everyday world and presented to us as objects of contemplation. Architecture does not generally come with captions. Curators and historians are not often on hand to tell us what is unique about a particular building or why another is undoubtedly a masterpiece. We can buy guidebooks and follow architectural tours.

We can read about buildings and architects and curate our own expeditions. But a lot of the time – most of the time, in fact – we are on our own, left to our own devices, experiencing architecture in the here and now.

This book is written very much in that moment, in the experience of architecture in the everyday. It is, if not against interpretation, certainly against a certain kind of interpretation that stops us looking at the buildings we are using. It is about developing the vocabulary that Sontag suggested, one that allows us to look harder and experience more. It is not about ignoring the weight of history or expert guidance. Not exactly. But it will hopefully help to move us on from received wisdom so that we can start to make critical judgements of our own.

Architecture and History

How do we do this? And how do we separate an enjoyment of architecture from the weight of its history or the circumstances of its birth? How can we discuss architecture as distinct from its social and urban context? And do we really have to separate buildings from this context, isolate them from the rest of life, in order to enjoy them?

On one level, architecture should be considered within the historical circumstances in which buildings are commissioned and built. It would be hard to look at a large eighteenth-century English country house, for example, and not wonder where the wealth to create such a lavish home came from. This is part of looking at and learning about architecture too. I see nothing undermining to architecture in trying to understand where great buildings come from. It might involve uncomfortable truths about wealth, exploitation and inequality, but this is not something we should shy away from. Enjoying architecture is not an excuse for wanting to brush unpalatable facts under the carpet. It is not a euphemism for uncritical consumption or simplistic stories, either.

In many ways, these complexities add to the enjoyment of architecture. They are part of its meaning. Buildings are expensive undertakings. Generally, they are built by people with the money, influence and power to commission them. Sometimes this is the state, sometimes it is a group or an organisation and sometimes it is an individual. In this sense, architecture is often regarded as a representation of privilege and prestige. Architecture is in many ways inherently conservative. It is often about consolidation, making temporary things more permanent and enshrining existing values. Architecture is also about property and who owns what.

The influential early twentieth-century Viennese architect Adolf Loos wrote: 'The work of art is revolutionary, but the house is conservative.' Loos defined a split between art's impulse to attack convention and architecture's desire to accommodate it. Architecture is nearly always commissioned, and architects nearly always have clients. This makes them different from artists. These are generalisations, of course. Architects sometimes make designs without a client in order to experiment with ideas. And artists sometimes work to order, producing art they have been commissioned to do. But the distinction generally holds, and it is part of what adds to the complexity of architecture as an art form that has multiple and sometimes conflicting motives. The American architect and writer Robert Venturi referred to this as 'the difficult whole'. He observed how architecture pulls in different directions, between practical and creative demands, between order and pragmatism, between art and the everyday.

This book includes great architecture and famous buildings, but it is also about more everyday structures and ordinary things. Partly this is because these can be beautifully and thoughtfully designed too, but it also because they are just as important to our experience of everyday life. Understanding that everything can contain a quality of thought and care in how it is designed and put together is important.

The examples used in the book are not always canonical – that is, part of the established chronology of the history of architecture. Instead, they reflect my own experience and therefore, hopefully, reflect the way that architecture is experienced more generally.

This book offers a way of understanding and experiencing the architecture that already exists. It is written in the belief that architecture might take you to other places or give insight into specific times or cultures or practices, but that this is not its main point or its responsibility. In a way the book is an argument against responsibility, too, an argument for enjoying the visual, spatial and material richness of buildings without a sense of guilt as to whether it is the right kind of architecture to like.

This is not to divorce architecture from its social and political circumstances, nor to deny the conditions in which it is made. I am not trying to place architecture in a gallery devoid of context. But something of the act of looking at art, of experiencing forms, materials and structures as physical objects, is important. Architecture has qualities that are also intrinsic to architecture. Sometimes it is what it is.

Architecture and Taste

Part of the motivation in writing this book was a frustration with the somewhat tribal and partisan way that buildings are often discussed. A binary opposition between modernism and classicism – reduced to their most cartoonish qualities – characterises much online discussion. A current staple on X (formerly Twitter), for instance, are posts that rely on an opposition of two images, one invariably of a classical building and one of a modernist one. The post's author usually makes it very clear which one we are supposed to like more. The tweet will say something like, 'When did we exchange the desire for beauty with ugliness?'

Subtler forms of this argument persist across architecture – and within it. Secular infighting characterises a lot of architectural debate. My aim here is not to enter into an argument for one kind of architecture over another. Nevertheless, the division of architecture into supposedly obvious categories of beauty and ugliness needs challenging if we are to approach buildings with a desire to appreciate them better and accept that even buildings we might not initially like do have merits.

An example close to (my) home might help to illustrate this. I frequently walk along the seafront of Dover, on the East Kent coast. The town sits in a wide stretch of harbour between two banks of white chalk cliffs. It is a famous view, familiar to many. The ferry port dominates the eastern edge, a complex logistical space managing the ceaseless movement of lorries on and off the boats. Beyond, the esplanade is dominated by two large buildings, one from the early eighteenth century and one from the mid-twentieth (fig. 1).

The earlier building is Waterloo Crescent, actually three white stucco blocks that curve gently with the profile of the beach. Waterloo

FIG. 1 Dover seafront showing Waterloo Crescent and the Gateway flats.

Crescent was designed by Philip Hardwick in the 1830s. It is a Grade II listed building, protected and preserved as an important example of Georgian seaside architecture. The later building is called the Gateway and consists of two large blocks of apartments. Completed in 1960, the Gateway is predominantly seven storeys high and runs parallel with the seafront. It is not listed and it is not particularly popular in Dover, routinely being described in local newspapers and on social media as an eyesore and a blot on the landscape.

Why is one building generally well liked and the other not? On the face of it this is – as they say – a no-brainer. It is not just ordinary people saying they prefer one rather than the other. This choice is seemingly endorsed by higher authorities and the official arbiters of taste, including Historic England. The Gateway flats are not listed. Waterloo Crescent is. There is apparently very little to discuss. Nothing to see here. End of.

But I am not completely happy with this explanation. I want to know what motivates our choices and what underlies our preferences. I want to question those preferences, too. But I want to do this in the spirit of enjoying architecture more and, perhaps, condemning buildings a little less. I also like the Gateway flats and would like to rescue them from their ignominious fate as the whipping boy of Dover seafront, an easy target for those decrying the (relatively) modern age as a desecrator of historic towns.

We privilege some buildings over others for all sorts of reasons. But what I am interested in here, what I think it might be useful to do, is to try to move beyond these a priori positions and to really look at the buildings in question. This book hopes to place you in the here and now, in the everyday experience of buildings. We will cover lots of ground, literally and metaphorically, and we will look at buildings from all over the world. But the intention is always the same: to approach those buildings as if they are in front of us and to foreground experience and observation over prior knowledge or assumed aesthetic preference.

So here we are, in the here and now, standing on Dover's slightly windswept seafront. There are undoubtedly some underlying ideological reasons accounting for the difference in the reactions to these two buildings. And opinions are not quite as clear as they first seem. Let's test the hypothesis of this introduction and look a little more, push our assumptions around a bit and test our prejudices.

Waterloo Crescent is a very good example of Regency seaside architecture. Other seaside towns that developed in the nineteenth century have a lot more of this kind of architecture: Brighton, for example, with its long, cream-coloured terraces rippling along the seafront. Dover doesn't have much. It grew as a port rather than a resort and it was very heavily bombed in the Second World War, so Waterloo Crescent is a rare local example.

Georgian urbanism tends towards the repetitive. It follows a system – of proportions, materials and details: a pattern book that could be used everywhere. The Georgians cared little for ideas about the vernacular or for local materials or appropriate scale or any of the other things we consider important in developments today. As a building, Waterloo Crescent is pretty much all façade. The rear elevation is a bit gloomy and makeshift: small windows and service entrances predominate. But the seafront is special. It is a long curving drumroll of an elevation alleviated by cross-rhythms of windows, awnings and balconies. It is a set piece, a showstopper, a big-band finale. It is not particularly subtle, but it is very effective. It is covered in white stucco, the very definition of seaside gaiety, its surface reflecting the light and standing clear and bright against the blue skies, when we have them.

How can the Gateway rival this? Isn't it just a big monster of repetitive flats and unrelieved brown brickwork? Well, for some reasonably objective reporting we could turn to *The Buildings of England*, that vast compendium of architecture listed county by county and initiated by the German-British art historian Nikolaus Pevsner. Specifically, we need to read the East Kent volume, written by John Newman, Pevsner's former assistant.

Newman describes the Gateway flats as more of a missed opportunity than a calamitous mistake. We are told that their balconies have a rather flat rhythm and that the taller, nine-storey block sits unhappily against the lower, longer section. The brown brick is also, apparently, a little dull. Along one section of the building, the one facing the town, the architects placed a row of prosaic and utilitarian garages. Newman is not entirely wrong. Some of this is true. But against this one could say that the white metal balconies have something celebratory about them. They stand out more strongly because of the relative dullness of the brick, and their long horizontal rhythms have an elegant 1950s quality reminiscent of the Festival of Britain. There is also a large, three-storey hole in the centre of the block which allows views through from the approaching street to the beach and the blue skies beyond. It is a dramatic moment, forming a raised piazza with the building bridging over it.

The gardens in front of the Gateway are in the tradition of ornamental seaside gardens everywhere. They have palm trees and decorative planting, and their scale is generous and inclusive: anyone can wander through them or take a seat and watch the ferry boats slowly come into the harbour, turn around and leave again.

Dover seafront has seen far greater crimes than the Gateway flats. Some of them are being built as I write. And seafronts tend to attract speculative developments of hotels and apartments, each one craning for that all-important view. Unlike most of these, the Gateway was built by the local authority as ordinary housing, which might also be part of the problem. Social housing is not meant to have the best views and it is certainly not meant to block the views of other people. So the Gateway has committed two crimes, one aesthetic and one cultural.

A regular criticism of the Gateway is that it destroys views of the seafront. It is not a gateway at all, but a barrier. In an obvious sense, this is true. It is a big building, and if you are standing on the town side of it, the sea is very much on the other. But the same criticism could be made of Waterloo Crescent, which dominates the other end of the seafront just as surely as the Gateway. Both these buildings effectively form the seafront, the edge of the town, defining views from the water. Neither building tries very hard to break down its mass or appear to be smaller than it really is.

So our objections to buildings might be the result of a complex mix of motivations, some aesthetic but others to do with who built them or who they are supposed to be for. History undoubtedly obscures this, lending older buildings a sense of permanence and a right to be where they are, whatever the motivations of those who put them there to start with. Cycles of fashion and taste therefore matter too when thinking about buildings. There is nothing as toxic as the recently fashionable, wrote the American artist Dan Graham. The Gateway is a building that comes from a period only now being reassessed for the quality of its architecture. Other buildings in Dover have not been so lucky.

A few yards along the front from the Gateway is a surface car park that was once the site of a building that the *Buildings of England* volume really did approve of: the Stage Hotel designed by Louis Erdi in 1957. Historical photographs of this building reveal something dynamic, sprightly, slender and vivacious. The Stage's five storeys of hotel rooms were perched jauntily on V-shaped concrete legs. The rooms – hoisted up in the air over a two-storey restaurant and reception building – were angled towards the sea. In front of the hotel Erdi designed an equally delightful garden, the whole composition having the conscious quality of a piece of American 'Googie' architecture: exuberant roadside buildings intended to grab the attention of motorists.

Erdi's remarkable building was demolished in the 1980s along with an equally audacious car showroom just a few yards away on the opposite side of the same street. Very few people mourn the loss of either building. It is possible that the demolition of such architecture – good-quality twentieth-century modernism – doesn't fit the narrative around conservation which presumes it is generally older buildings that need conserving and modern ones that we need protecting from.

The question this generates, though, is important: how do we value and judge buildings that are unpopular at certain points in history? Which ones do we like and why? Undoubtedly our reaction to buildings is culturally generated: we learn to some extent which buildings to like and which to dislike. We breathe in an atmosphere made up of stories and myths around architecture that are part of the cultural landscape we inhabit.

This landscape is not continuous or neutral, and neither is our role in it. Different social and cultural classes tend to like different kinds of buildings for different reasons. In the case of Dover's Gateway flats, questions of wider social and political value hover over our opinion of the building, fusing with aesthetic prejudice.

So this book has another aim, which is to move beyond received opinion and popular prejudice and to really look at buildings. This might mean we look at some that are considered a bit beyond the pale. My purpose is not to try to convince anyone of the merits of, say, the Gateway over Waterloo Crescent, or to stoke the flames of an already incendiary culture war. I would prefer to see both as worthy of interest. And so this book is partly about the question of how we judge buildings and how opinions of them are established. It is also written in the hope that some of these judgements might change, or at least become more open to reinterpretation. One way of enjoying architecture is to be less judgemental and more interested.

Structure: What Not to Expect

This is not a history of architecture. Nor is it a book that promotes one style of architecture over another. The history of architecture can often be seen as a history of stylistic battles and manifestos, of dos and don'ts and diktats about the right way to build. Walk through any town and you'll see that these debates manifest themselves in Gothic Revival town halls, mock-Tudor houses, neo-Palladian touches on new estates, Brutalist car parks or a hint of Arts and Crafts detailing in a suburban street. But this book won't tell you which of these styles of architecture is the best.

The aim here is rather to point to the pleasures of very different styles and periods and to identify the qualities that contribute to the satisfying symmetry of a Queen Anne house, the thrill of a high-tech office block or the clever ideas behind a 1960s housing estate. When designed with intelligence and care, all buildings can enrich our lives and provide profound pleasure. Learning something about the styles, materials and compositional qualities of architecture makes the enjoyment of architecture accessible to everyone. Understanding the role of structure doesn't sound like fun, but recognising what materials are doing what and how things stand up or support each other is an important part of 'reading' buildings. Most of all, it is how these various things connect that is important. Buildings are complicated, technical things but they are also ones that we meet every day, again and again and in countless ways.

This is not an encyclopaedia or a global survey. I make no pretence to having a comprehensive understanding of architecture. Inevitably, many buildings, eras, spaces and places will go unmentioned. I have taken examples from here and there: buildings experienced many times over and some visited perhaps just once or twice. The book is based on my knowledge and enthusiasms and it is intended to place the reader in the here and now, within the experience of visiting or using a piece of architecture. Sometimes I talk about buildings I have not actually visited and know only through photographs and drawings. Part of my experience as an architect is to study photographs and look at drawings and learn to understand aspects of buildings from secondary sources. This, after all, is what architects do when they design. Architects produce drawings and models of buildings, not the buildings themselves. We learn to project ideas and qualities about buildings before they physically exist. I have tried to impart some of the enjoyment of this, too.

One last but very important point in relation to the issue of which buildings, architects and places have been included. Architecture is necessarily going through a vital process of deconstructing many of its own assumptions. Architectural history is not neutral, and the privileging of some people, societies and civilisations represents centuries of prejudice and power. Again, this is not something to shy away from. The canon of architecture has generally been a history populated by men – and white, Western men at that. I have tried to break out of this at points and to tell a more inclusive story.

This is not, though, an attempt to rewrite the history of architecture. Others are engaged in this process, and it is undoubtedly a necessary one. This book uses examples not to hold them up as unquestionable works of genius but as examples of ideas that help to illuminate aspects of architecture that I think are useful or important. Some may disagree with the choices but will hopefully still find the observations interesting, useful and helpful. They are intended as examples of how to experience architecture that can be applied to other buildings and other places and therefore add to an enjoyment of it more generally.

Structure: What to Expect

The book is divided into a series of chapters that focus on key aspects of architecture: Style, Composition, Space, Materials, Structure and Use. Each chapter is intended to help us understand what we are looking at when we look at a building and to equip us with the tools and skills to better enjoy them.

The book starts with style – the most visually obvious aspects of architecture – and works backwards to describe how buildings are put together, organised, made to stand up and used. Each chapter is primarily about our everyday experience of architecture, about what we can see and readily understand rather than about complex technical issues.

It is important to say too that 'looking' really means the full range of sensory experience available to us when we inhabit buildings. Looking includes smell, touch and sound but it also means the codes of behaviour and the hierarchies of activity that inform our reactions. When we go into a library, we are conditioned to act differently to when we pass through a busy train station. But we can all learn to exercise a critical faculty, to step back in order to compare, examine, read and enjoy the spaces we inhabit and the buildings that are all around us.

Some of these chapters might appear at first glance more straight-forward than others. Most of us have a sense of what architectural style means. We might be able to distinguish a Gothic building from a classical one or understand how modernism differs from post-modernism. But space is a particularly thorny and elusive concept. It is a word that architects use a lot and – in my experience – one that other people don't. At least in relation to buildings.

Similarly, structure is quite a specialist topic, something most obviously bound up with technical demands and engineering knowledge. But this is a book about how to enjoy architecture and therefore each of these topics is approached in the same way – that is, with a view to describing how they add to our experience of buildings in a non-specialist sense. The chapter on structure is no more technical than the one on style. Some specialist language will inevitably be involved, but for the most part I have tried to avoid jargon and the problem of sailing too far into technical backwaters.

The list of chapters is not definitive. I am sure that readers will ask why these elements and not others. What of colour, for instance, or decoration? These do appear and they are a large part of what I enjoy about architecture. But I have chosen to weave them into the main categories I have settled on. To tackle them as separate elements would have meant heading into very specific and arcane territory, too – aspects of historical definition and lineage that would be beyond the scope of this particular book.

I could have broken architecture down into the constituent parts of a building: doors, stairs, elevators, windows, floors, etc. But this felt reductive: a shopping list of parts rather than a sense of how buildings work more holistically. So the chapters are deliberately broad and cover ideas and how these ideas inform buildings. Architecture might be composed of stairs and walls and windows, but what I am most interested in here is what it means to compose a building to start with. The focus is not so much on what architects do but what results from that doing. How does it affect the buildings we use, visit and experience?

Each chapter uses examples of buildings and architects to help explore its theme. These aren't chronological and they range freely across different times, styles, countries and continents. I have tried to be eclectic in my choices, but inevitably my own tastes and interests – as well as the limitations of my knowledge and experience – shape the journey. It is important to restate that this book is not a conventional history of architecture. It is not exhaustive or encyclopaedic by any means, and it relies on my personal experience and judgement of architecture. It is not a whistle-stop tour through architecture, either. At the end of it the reader won't be able to rattle off a potted history of modern architecture or recite all the major architects of the Renaissance period. Nor is it about stylistic preferences – I have very few axes to grind in stylistic terms, and so this is not an argument in favour of modernism over classicism or traditional rather than contemporary architecture.

When I started studying architecture in the early 1990s, I had already read a little about it. I was interested in architecture as a battle of styles, and I thought my history of architecture lectures would be about that. My first theory teacher was a very softly spoken man named Robin Evans, who will make several appearances in this book. Robin Evans began my first ever history and theory lecture by stating that he was uninterested in revisiting the generally accepted history of architecture and the conventions of reading it as a series of stylistic battles. Initially my heart sank. What on earth was architectural history if not that?

Instead, Evans's lectures took odd, sometimes random-seeming loose threads of history and thought, and followed them into strange and unexpected places. He talked about architecture in ways I had never thought about and opened up the subject in ways that still influence my work and ideas. His lectures were a constant surprise, but they always started from an observation, or a detail based on his experience.

I hope this book achieves a measure of his approach. It is grounded in my own experience of looking at and, of course, designing buildings, and it aims to place the reader in a direct relationship with architecture, not as an abstract discipline or a list of names and places but as an experience. This experience is both mental and physical. We inhabit buildings with our bodies, following their layouts, letting handrails guide us upstairs and the position of windows direct our gaze. Small rooms place us in intimate relationships with objects and with other people; large and spectacular rooms can stop us in our tracks. We might seek out the cool of a cathedral when in hot cities or the warmth of a pub on a cold night.

The physical effects of architecture are easier to describe than its conceptual ones. Yet buildings engage us intellectually, too. Most obviously this might be when they carry specific information in the form of sculpture or art. Last summer I was in Assisi, and I visited the Church of St Francis. Inside, the walls of the church are lined with frescoes by Giotto and I wandered through it in a daze of information and imagery, trying to soak it all up, to understand the stories being depicted.

This is precisely the kind of experience the writer of an architecture book is meant to describe. It is not made up – I really did go to Assisi and I really was transfixed by the space and the paintings. But I was on holiday, visiting a site acknowledged generally as a masterpiece of pre-Renaissance art, a place of pilgrimage in every sense.

What of the everyday, the ordinary experiences of architecture, the petty or minor navigations of buildings we live in and work in or visit for specific needs? Is architecture worthy of our attention then? How do we experience it when rushing down a busy high street or navigating a shopping mall? Are we supposed to be thinking about it when going about our normal, everyday business in normal, everyday places?

There are buildings and places we are prepared to give time to and situations when we are more primed for aesthetic experiences. Normally this is when we have the time and are in situations where we have chosen to relax or to experience art and architecture – on holiday, usually, but maybe too on a special night out, at an expensive dinner or on a visit to a country house or an art gallery.

These occasions and experiences are important, and they acknowledge something about the role of architecture in our lives. But what are we supposed to make of these isolated encounters? How do we connect them up? Should we even bother? What buildings and examples of architecture are important to pay attention to? How do we know when we are looking at architecture?

I spend a lot of time looking at architecture. It is my job, after all. I am fascinated by it. I notice it when I am walking around, in the here and now. But I will also travel to see it. I like visiting new places, observing the patterns and forms and materials of the architecture in it. This is not always good. I get depressed by bad architecture and angry when cynicism or lack of care results in ugly buildings that make our environment worse in some way.

But this book is not about that: not directly, at least. In hoping to engage a greater interest in buildings and an enjoyment of architecture, I have, I admit, a secret wish that this might improve things, mean that cynical and venal buildings will be harder to get away with. That might be a happy accident or a fortunate side-effect. But the main point, the ambition of this book, is to open up an experience of architecture as something enlightening and educational but also enjoyable: to communicate some of the pleasure that I get from looking at architecture and good buildings.

This involves exploring buildings but also examining the ideas that led to them. We will talk about style, although not exhaustively. We will also talk about composition and space – a favourite word of architects – and use, materials and structure. We will cover how consideration of these things leads to certain kinds of buildings and how buildings are effectively an amalgam of multiple considerations. Buildings are complicated things that serve a lot of roles. In a way it is remarkable that they manage to be beautiful or elegant or aesthetically thoughtful at all. But it is through the reconciliation of multiple requirements that they become fascinating: the way they resolve lots of different things into a coherent whole, an object that works on multiple levels.

The individual chapters in this book, then, represent the main critical issues that buildings need to address and that architects think about the most when designing them. More than resolving them, though, the most successful buildings manage to say something new about them, to push aspects of them forward or at least in new or unexpected directions. Buildings contain ideas. And so, finally, this book is about ideas too. It is about the ideas that lead to buildings and the ideas that they generate. In opening our experience of buildings, we might enjoy those ideas, too.

CHAPTER I

Style

T HE history of Western architecture is often seen as a history of styles. Some of us might be familiar with the roll call: Palladian, Gothic, modernist, Brutalist, etc. These styles are generally held to represent different periods in time, with changes in style reflecting wider changes in society. But the truth is inevitably more complicated than that, with styles mutating and recurring throughout architectural history. Inevitably, discussing architecture in terms of style can seem reductive, an attempt to pin neat labels onto complex objects and circumstances. Is modernism – the dominant mode of architecture of the twentieth century – usefully described as a style? Or is it part of a much broader impulse for architecture to reflect radical changes in society?

In architectural theory, style can sometimes be seen as a pejorative term, something superficial and secondary to more important issues such as the use or the materiality of a building. This chapter is written in the belief that style *is* important and that it forms a critical aspect of how we understand and approach architecture. It can offer a profound way in to enjoying buildings and a vital component of how they communicate. Style is one way of describing why buildings look the way they do.

I have tried to avoid the usual way of writing about style as a chronological history of neatly defined categories. Instead, this chapter is about buildings that sometimes mix styles and about styles that blur into different eras or that return after a period in the wilderness.

Looking at style in this way means that we can see it as something that can be chosen deliberately: it might be used at any time, even if its origins lie far in the past. I could perhaps have used the word character rather than style. What is the character of a building? Why is it appropriate? Why has the architect chosen it? Was it a deliberate choice or the result of other pressures such as money, planning, the taste of the client? Why do buildings look the way they do?

The Monstrous Carbuncle

A term that is used a lot when discussing new buildings is 'fitting in'. It is generally regarded as a good thing to 'fit in'. All sorts of ideas of harmony – visual and social – are bound up with this. But the history of architecture includes many styles, often in the same place. Walk along a high street and you are likely to see a wide array of different styles of buildings from different eras. So how do we decide what the right style is, and is that the same as the building immediately next door? Let's start with looking at a controversial building, one that exposes a lot of preconceptions and prejudices about style.

The Sainsbury Wing in London's Trafalgar Square (fig. 2) is an extension to the National Gallery. The gallery's original building, designed by William Wilkins, was completed in 1838 to house the national collection of artworks. It is built of stone in the neo-classical style. That is to say, it is a nineteenth-century building that draws heavily on Greek and Roman antecedents to form an architecture based on the use of the 'orders', a system of columns, mouldings and proportions.

Despite its cultural importance and prominent position in Trafalgar Square, Wilkins's gallery has never been considered an especially great building in architectural circles. This is because, in terms of neo-classicism, it is not a particularly strong composition.

FIG. 2 Sainsbury Wing, National Gallery, London.

Despite its size, it is not imposing, and its low, flat frontage is a little rambling. The quality of its mouldings – the relief designs that enliven façades – and its decoration are routine rather than inspired. Nonetheless, it is a building that has come to represent British culture in many ways, and it inspires a certain amount of affection. While not brilliant, it does its job.

In 1982, an architectural competition was organised to extend the National Gallery. This new gallery was to house the nation's collection of early Renaissance art. The competition was won by ABK, a well-established British practice named after its three partners, Peter Ahrends, Richard Burton and Paul Koralek. ABK's design was forcefully and unambiguously modernist. It contained very few references to classical architecture: no columns, mouldings or applied decoration.

Instead, the design referred to the early twentieth-century modernism of Russian Constructivism, an architecture that expressed its structure via industrial elements. ABK's building referred not to ancient Greece or imperial Rome, but to the revolutionary art and architecture of the early twentieth century. While not rejecting the architecture of William Wilkins's building, it wanted to be very clearly different from it. The design also accommodated uses that were not traditionally part of an art gallery, including a large amount of commercial office space.

The design was infamously denounced by the then Prince Charles at a speech made at the invitation of the Royal Institute of British Architecture in 1984. The RIBA had not asked Prince Charles to attack ABK's design or modern architecture more generally, and his combative speech took everyone by surprise. He described the design for the National Gallery extensions as 'a monstrous carbuncle on the face of a much-loved friend'.

Whatever one thinks of Prince Charles's intervention, it was an effective turn of phrase, one that has become a popular form for denouncing buildings ever since (the construction industry newspaper, *Building Design*, used to award an annual prize for the worst building of the year called the Carbuncle Cup). The immediate effect was to derail the design, leading eventually to the project's cancellation.

A subsequent competition was run and a new and very different design was selected in 1985. The financial support of the Sainsbury family meant that the new extension no longer had to include office space and could be purely focused on exhibition spaces. The winning proposal – designed by the American practice of Venturi, Scott Brown & Associates (VSBA) – was eventually built and has proved just as controversial, but for very different reasons.

VSBA's design is an example of postmodernism, an architectural style made popular (if not actually named) by the American critic Charles Jencks. Postmodernism, as its name suggests, was a partial rejection of modernism, a style that developed as a reaction to what was perceived as modernism's limitations. Modernism – it was felt – was too harsh, too brutal and too insensitive. People – by which critics meant ordinary people – didn't understand it, so they often did not like it.

The Sainsbury Wing looks, at first glance, to be much more closely related to William Wilkins's building than ABK's one. It is faced in stone, for one thing: the same stone as the National Gallery. And it has classical columns. The windows – which are punched out of the façade in the same way that classical ones are – have the same proportions and are vertical in aspect rather than horizontal. They have a rhythm and spacing that also relates to the older building. While ABK's proposal featured a tower, the Sainsbury Wing and the National Gallery are very noticeably the same height.

There are, though, some key but subtle differences. If the main elements – material, height, window style – are about fitting in, looking the same as the main building, the differences are subtle but insistent. Look hard at the Sainsbury Wing and you can see that it is more similar where it joins the National Gallery than it is further away. It seems to start off the same and then slowly mutate into something else. The columns get more widely spaced and less expressed until they start to disappear altogether. The same thing happens with the windows. And unlike Wilkins's building, the front façade of the Sainsbury isn't flat. It is folded, almost as if a sheet of cardboard with a classical building drawn on it had been bent to go around a corner. This bending does odd things to the classical language of architecture, which is more generally used on flat façades. It makes it strange and slightly unsettling, a little like one of Salvador Dalí's melting watches.

Finally, the façade seems to have large holes in it, openings at ground level that don't appear to be doors or ways in so much as dark voids punched out. It is as if someone has taken a bit of Wilkins's façade, folded it up, cut bits out of it and then stuck it onto a very differently shaped building. It is similar but also very odd. And because a lot of people tell us that the VSBA building is conservative and looks too much like the older, original building next door, we tend to overlook the bits about it that aren't similar. It is as if it has turned up to an event looking ostensibly right, in the correct sort of outfit, only to reveal it is not wearing any trousers.

As you get closer to it, you realise more things that aren't right. These things tend to be bits of architecture – styles – that we weren't expecting: neo-Egyptian columns and sections of what looks suspiciously like a modernist 'curtain wall' of glass, for example. And as you walk around the building, moving from Trafalgar Square to the start of Pall Mall and then further round the back to St Martin's Street, the building changes with it. It shifts material from stone to brick. The windows change proportion from vertical to horizontal. The classical nods have gone at this point, and have been replaced by references to other periods of architecture: Victorian warehouses, art deco cinemas, modernist office blocks.

The Sainsbury Wing is a great starting point to talk about architectural styles because it combines so many in one place. It is a chameleon, changing its character to reflect the neighbouring streets and the shifting role of the gallery to them. This is also why it is disliked, particularly by architects and architectural critics who regard this shifting character as duplicitous, untrustworthy and the sign of a failure of nerve. Buildings should not copy their surroundings, they suggest. They should strongly and clearly and unapologetically reflect the era in which they were built and the materials and techniques of their age. This strange, sliding impersonation of multiple styles and eras just isn't right.

So the Sainsbury Wing undermines any one style's claim to authority by demonstrating that all styles are about choice and that buildings can move between them. It also disassociates style from any one historical period. The idea that architecture expresses its own times is a powerful one. It sounds, on the face of it, extremely obvious. Of course it should! How could it not? And yet style and the decisions over how a building looks are always open to manipulation and choice.

The architecture critic Reyner Banham once described postmodernism as 'architecture in drag'. It is a revealing comment, not least because of what it implies about Banham's own prejudices. It assumes that just as there is a proper way for men or women to dress, there is a proper way for architecture to look, one that confirms and establishes clear categories. In this sense, blurring those categories, playing with our expectations and certainties, is challenging and even radical. The Sainsbury Wing is all about style. It wants to wear many different outfits at once, changing style and character at will. Paradoxically, it may want to do this not to stand out but in order to fit in.

I am not necessarily claiming that the Sainsbury Wing is a radical building. But it is a very interesting one. It uses architectural style as a way to be acceptable. But it does so with such slippery ease and with such artful duplicity that it can only bring our attention to the malleability of such conceits. Style here is no longer a logical consequence of the correct way to build but a dressing-up box of opportunity.

The Right Styles for the Job

So one way of talking about style in architecture might be to look at buildings that use more than one, that see style as substance. Style gives buildings meaning; it offers a way for them to speak and to say things about where they are, who they are for and what they are about. But it might also be a way to say more than one thing or to say several different things at the same time. Style in this sense becomes more of a conversation, or perhaps a play of conversations and a way of negotiating different ideas or needs.

The Sainsbury Wing is one example of a building that changes style or that wants to be more than one style at a time. Homewood, by Edwin Lutyens (fig. 3), is another. Built on the Knebworth estate in Hertfordshire in 1903 for Lutyens's mother-in-law, Homewood is an exercise in using competing architectural styles to tell a satirical story. Like the contemporary stories of the satirist H.H. Munro (Saki), it is an exercise in brittle irony and barbed social commentary.

Approached along a driveway through a wood, the house presents itself at first as a country cottage: the front elevation consists of three steep gables clad in horizontal timber boarding with small, leaded casement windows. There are clues, though, in this apparently humble, rustic façade, that other games are afoot. The timber cladding stops at first-floor level to reveal a stucco base coursed with horizontal incisions to resemble stonework. And in the centre of the façade sits an elaborate classical doorcase. Like much of the house, this doorcase is a deceit, a clue that is also a red herring. The doorway turns out not to be the front door but an opening leading into a mysterious passage. The actual front door is somewhere at the back of the passage, hidden in darkness and easily mistaken for

FIG. 3 Homewood, Hertfordshire, designed by Edwin Lutyens.

the door to a broom cupboard. It introduces visitors to the first of many complexities in Lutyens's confounding plan.

The subtle but insistent symmetry of the front elevation and its elaborate doorway offers strong hints that this is not a country cottage at all, but a much more ambitious piece of classical architecture. The rear, garden façade of Homewood is neither rustic nor classical but the apparent result of an intense wrestling match between the two. The roof, with its hand-made clay peg tiles, sweeps down low towards the garden at the sides, but in the middle, it is lifted up to reveal a classical elevation with four tall Ionic columns seemingly holding it aloft. It is as if a classical villa has been hidden inside a vernacular cottage, with all the attendant subversions of expectation and experience that this would entail.

The 'style' of Homewood is not purely classical or vernacular but mannerist, a derivation of classicism that subverts its formal language. It is a style within a style, but – in both Lutyens's and VSBA's use – it is also a set of tactics for playing games with expectations and rules. Mannerism relies on a well-established set of rules, which can then be messed around with. The classical language of architecture lends itself to mannerism because its language is so highly developed and so strict. This strictness leads to mild acts of insurrection. Lutyens designed a lot of buildings in the mannerist mode, introducing rules and expectations only to undermine them. Symmetry is sometimes carefully set up and then undermined by a deliberately unsymmetrical moment. Views and formal approaches are subverted by blank walls or dead ends – as in Homewood's front door – and radically different styles of architecture are placed in uneasy relationships.

At Homewood, Lutyens sets up an expectation of sweet, vernacular pleasures – a simple, homely architecture of timber-clad gables and little casement windows – only to reveal a grander, more formal architecture lurking within. The two are in a creatively unresolved tension with each other, much like the tension one imagines in the

relationship of Lutyens with his mother-in-law about the kind of
house she wanted to live in. Perhaps her preference was for something formal and impressive which Lutyens felt unsuitable for the
site. Or perhaps she wanted a relaxing, unpretentious cottage which
Lutyens couldn't quite bring himself to design, choosing instead
to smuggle in moments of 'high' architecture. Or perhaps she was
in on the joke(s), keen to send herself up or enjoy the paradoxes
of her own social position as the 'dowager' of a vast country estate,
displaced from the main house by her own children. Whatever her
role in its design, by all accounts the Countess of Lytton disliked
her house, finding it cold and dark.

Despite this, Homewood's brilliance as a piece of architecture
rests on the degree to which it combines different styles, different
registers, with a high degree of wit and irony. If Homewood is
about fitting in, it is more in the social than the architectural sense.
One could say that it is contextual – a cottage in the woods – in
the broad, cultural sense of the expectations we have about architecture. It takes a style we might assume is right for the site and
then slowly, subtly and with subversive intent reveals one that isn't.
In doing so, it seems to say something sly and sardonic about its
owner and their status.

Style here is again something identified with expectations of
social standing and aspiration. The mixing of classical and vernacular
styles, though, unbalances that aspiration, rendering it precarious
and exposing its conceits. It is like a carefully constructed accent
slipping. You could say that Homewood is not much more than an
elaborate parlour game – literally as well as metaphorically. Lutyens
took the acceptable, aspirational architectural styles favoured by
his clients and played games with them, subverted their rules and
brought in things that he liked, or thought that they should like.
Lutyens chose the right style for the job and then mixed it with the
wrong ones. Style – in a Lutyens building – is an elaborate formal
game and a sophisticated form of social commentary.

Style as Non-Style

If the Sainsbury Wing and Homewood are examples of buildings that seem to want to fit in – albeit in ways that are sometimes oblique or ironic – what would be an example of one that doesn't, one that really, really wants to stand out? And how should we judge such a building? In a sense, the linear, chronological idea of architectural history – as a series of stylistic ruptures, radical shifts in style – is a history of not fitting in. Style can be a way of reconciling different expectations, but it can also be a way of manifesting difference by creating an explosion, a moment of profound change.

The Centre Pompidou in Paris (fig. 4) was officially completed in 1977. It is named after Georges Pompidou – the president of France from 1969 to 1974 – and houses the Bibliothèque Publique d'Information along with the Musée National d'Art Moderne and IRCAM, a centre for music and acoustic research. The finished building was the result of an international design competition,

FIG. 4 Centre Pompidou, Paris, designed by Renzo Piano and Richard Rogers.

launched in 1970, that received nearly 700 entries. It was won by a youthful architectural practice, formed for the purposes of entering the competition, led by two architects: Richard Rogers and Renzo Piano.

Their design is routinely described as radical, revolutionary even. It certainly doesn't look like anything else around it. The centre of Paris is particularly uniform in architectural style, the result of a comprehensive rebuilding by Baron Haussmann between 1853 and 1870. Into Haussmann's consistent city streets of five-storey, stone-faced, baroque buildings, Piano and Rogers dropped an explosion of pipes, ducts, air vents and external escalators loosely held together within a vast steel exoskeleton. The building has been likened to an oil rig, a giant Meccano set and even a nuclear power station mid-meltdown.

The Centre Pompidou was controversial from the start. Its arrival in Paris aroused considerable antipathy and it continues to do so. There are a lot of justifications for its appearance and the supposed logic of its design. The designers have always been keen to claim that the externalising of mechanical plant, staircases and escalators makes the interior flexible and adaptable in a way that is presumably useful for an art gallery. The building is intended to be future-proof. It recognises that contemporary buildings are as much equipment as they are structures, and all that equipment often needs to change when it becomes redundant. Why not acknowledge this, and put the stuff that needs to change on the outside where you can get to it? Not only this, but at the Centre Pompidou, the internal walls and even floors can be moved, theoretically making it flexible and capable of adapting to different needs and requirements.

Despite serving a very similar function, this is a building that is the antithesis of Venturi, Scott Brown & Associates' Sainsbury Wing. It doesn't want to fit in. But it is not without history, or precedent. It doesn't come from nowhere. What is its style? We might call it an anti-style, although that comes with caveats. The justification for the Centre Pompidou from its architects and from its admirers is that it is functional. Its rationale is based on what it does, rather than what it looks like. It is an inside-out building that reverses the usual logic of architecture. And it does this in order to make a new kind of architecture, one not bound up in archaic ideas of façades and fenestration patterns, stone and brick and solid, load-bearing clumps of stuff. It is a building that comes from a tradition of architects attempting to escape what they saw as the trap of historic architecture – all that burdensome weight of history – and attempting instead to rethink the discipline and the technology of buildings.

The Centre Pompidou is simply not playing the same game as the buildings around it. The polite etiquette of aligning windows with your neighbour or using the same materials is irrelevant here. That is not to say that the building does not have a style, or that it is uninterested in questions of aesthetics. The Centre Pompidou is an extremely stylish building, in the sense both that it relates to a history of architectural style and that it does so in ways that are sophisticated and highly accomplished. This is most obvious in the flamboyance of its elements. Do those pipes need to be that large, for instance? Or be painted in such bright colours? Does the structure really need to be so vast, and so prominent?

No doubt there are localised justifications for these decisions – the Centre Pompidou's structural engineer, Peter Rice, became almost as famous as its architects (which is rare in the construction industry) – and the seemingly wilful extravagance has some basis in functional need. But the overall impression, the overwhelming character of this extraordinary building, is the need to express an idea in the most extreme and forceful way possible. The Centre Pompidou takes a logical idea about architecture and pushes it to an almost illogical conclusion. It is a tour de force, an absurd dream-like object, an utterly fantastic contraption.

Having doubts about the functional justification or internal logic of the Centre Pompidou is not to deny its formal power. It remains an extraordinary achievement and an exhilarating experience. It attempted to break away from the idea of architecture as a history of styles and in doing so established a style of its own. Its authors tried to hide its aesthetic radicalism behind a seemingly practical plea for a more flexible architecture. But who were they really trying to kid? Very few people remark on seeing the Centre Pompidou that its ducts must be easy to replace. To my knowledge the floors have never moved. These things are rhetorical, ultimately: elements expressed by the architects in the interests of a stylistic functionalism. We will talk about function – or use – in another chapter. It is enough to say here that style is a kind of function in itself. It serves a purpose, even when its role is to express an idea of functionality.

Richard Rogers went on to realise another, equally incredible building for Lloyd's of London. Lloyd's is like the Centre Pompidou after being twinned with a medieval cathedral, a vast, soaring, cyber-Gothic fantasy. Despite this extraordinary stylistic rhetoric, Rogers reached for the same justification as the Pompidou, claiming that the Lloyd's building's expressive concrete grid was easily extendable, as if this strange machine could spread across the city at the pull of a lever, its tubes and ducts hissing while disconnecting and reconnecting.

Rogers performed this trick of externalising a building's structure and services with slightly diminishing returns on many subsequent buildings. It became a house style, one that his later office Rogers Stirk Harbour (now RSH) still employs. The technique became so synonymous with Rogers that the satirical TV show *Spitting Image*, originally shown on UK television in the 1980s, used to have a puppet of Rogers which had its internal organs on the outside. It was a good joke. And it captured the paradox of Rogers's work, which was that an architecture that was not meant to be about style, an approach in fact that rejected the whole history of styles in favour of a purely technical understanding of buildings, became very, very stylish.

English high-tech was meant to be anti-style, an architecture that attempted to break away from the history of architecture and base itself in practical demands. But Rogers was not alone. Sliding incongruously into the streetscape of Downshire Hill, a road in north London made up of large, early Victorian villas, is the Hopkins House, a small, elegant, ethereal glass box. The house presents only a single-storey elevation to the street and so at first appears almost as a gap or an absence between its well-heeled, three- and four-storey neighbours. It is set back from the road by a sort of moat, and the house is accessed via a short metal bridge.

You enter at the first floor and a curving spiral stair takes you down to the garden level. The stair is in the centre of a plan that is highly minimal, pure space divided by glazed screens. The structure of the house is on show: a frame made from impossibly thin-looking steel columns and trusses. The exterior is clad in large glass panels and profiled steel sheeting. It is like a very tiny and very beautiful factory.

There are many interesting things about this house: the way that it combines a home and an office, the lack of conventional domestic planning and the resulting interplay of functions and uses. But the principal reason to mention it here is the way that it defines an architectural style, one that is entirely alien to its context. The house was designed by Michael and Patty Hopkins for themselves in the mid-1970s. The steel frame was made in a real factory on Canvey Island in the Thames estuary and brought to this affluent street like a visitor from somewhere alien. It is simply like nothing else there. And it is almost not there itself. It doesn't fit in. Instead, it attempts to play an entirely different game, nearly disappearing in the process.

That something so slight and so elegant might evolve from the language of industrial sheds and steel fabricators on Canvey Island is one of the inadvertent ironies of high-tech. Its architects took the nuts and bolts of industrial production and refined them into delicate, almost decorative elements. Lurking within the architecture of high-tech is an anti-architecture, a desire for the discipline to escape its own history and to become something lightweight, adaptable, transportable and extendable, a sophisticated service more than a building. English high-tech – the high-tech of Richard Rogers and the Hopkinses (at least in their earlier, purer phase, before the traditional materials of architecture got a hold on their imagination) – is a derivation of the work of architects such as Jean Prouvé and Buckminster Fuller, designers who were interested in ideas of mass production and industrial processes. Their architectural designs were prototypes, intended to be read as ideas, inventions even, the rough first drafts of something much greater.

Yet high-tech masterpieces such as the Hopkins House are one-off, bespoke objects. They may not have been conceived as such, but they were really ends in themselves, not harbingers of a new future for architecture but exceptional moments within its history. They have more in common with minimalist conceptual artists such as Donald Judd, turning the materials of heavy industry into elegantly poised objects. As an architectural style predicated on rejecting architectural style, high-tech was a resounding failure. But its failure is useful and interesting in trying to understand what style in architecture might mean.

The Queen Anne Revival Revival

I have already suggested that the idea of architectural style as a clear chronology – one style neatly following another – is a pervasive but problematic concept. The idea of the zeitgeist – a German compound word meaning, literally, the 'spirit of the age' – has a compelling logic. It implies that architectural styles reflect wider changes in society in ways that are both obvious and unarguable. New styles of buildings arrive and change the landscape and the language of architecture. There is a powerful pull to this line of thinking and a pleasing sense of advancement and progress. And when we look at a piece of architecture, it helps to have an approximate idea of when it was built. Buildings that try to look older than they are confound our understanding of architecture.

But the chronology of styles is rarely so simple, or so linear. So it is interesting to look at styles of architecture that come and go, sometimes persisting well beyond their supposed sell-by date. Neo-Georgian (or neo-Geo for short) is a good place to start. It is a style that, in art historical terms, has long outstayed its welcome.

Most of us are familiar with the neo-Geo architecture of contemporary housing developments. The style is easy to caricature, invariably made or clad in brick with fake sash windows, carriage lamps and maybe faux-stone classical columns around the front door. The more upmarket versions might have a flat-fronted parapet with stone trim or steps up to the front door with metal railings. The term is generally used in a pejorative manner, dismissing such aspirations as either vulgar or laughable pastiche.

In architectural circles, neo-Geo is generally regarded as a debased style, the kind of architecture that lacks authenticity or value. It is tempting to see it as an aberration, a disappointing retreat from modernism, the symptom of a failure of nerve or conviction. And yet neo-Geo has its own history. There have been a number of periods when it has been popular. As a style, it both predated modernism and existed alongside it. To the exasperation of many modernists, it was hugely popular in the inter-war period in the UK, used extensively for building programmes such as banks, libraries and municipal offices across the country.

Some architects associated with the development of modernism in the UK even managed to slip between the two styles. Oliver

Hill is one example. Hill was something of a shapeshifter anyway, an architect who moved between styles easily, depending on client and circumstance. Before the Second World War, he had been a more consistent proselytiser for modernism, an advocate of its supposed health-giving qualities: large windows, well-lit rooms, fresh air, balconies and roof terraces. He designed several pioneering modernist buildings in the UK, including the majestic, art deco Midland Hotel overlooking Morecambe Bay. The architectural historian Alan Powers has referred to his style somewhat waspishly as 'Vogue Regency', an art deco-inflected, chicly glamorous form of modernism, largely devoid of its more revolutionary aims.

Hill was responsible for planning a permanent settlement on the Essex coast called Frinton Park Village. This collection of flat-roofed, white-walled modernist houses epitomised the inter-war vogue for healthy living, combining sea views with expansive windows and roof terraces. Hill's original plan also included a long, elegantly curved hotel running along the cliff edge and overlooking the invigorating aspect of the North Sea. The hotel remained unbuilt, and the village was not – at least at first – a success, partly due to negative perceptions of the architecture from potential buyers. Perhaps because of this, Hill turned his hand to a gentler, neo-Geo style that was more closely attuned to the sensibilities of his well-heeled clients.

The presence of neo-Geo architecture alongside modernism obviously causes problems in relation to an argument that architecture should both express its age and search for the new and the contemporary. It is problematic in that it is an architectural style that refers explicitly to the buildings of a previous era, but it also blurs time and function in ways that can be confusing. Horace Field's buildings around Cowley Street (fig. 5) in London's Westminster, built in the early years of the twentieth century, are a good case in point. Here, Field employed a sophisticated and subtle form of architecture drawn from both the Queen Anne and the Georgian periods to form a street made up of offices that look like little eighteenth-century country houses joined together. The architecture is good, sumptuous even, with its deep red bricks, glassy white window frames and elaborate decorative doorcases. It could easily be 200 years older than it is, perhaps even designed by Sir Christopher Wren or one of his contemporaries. Field's work at Cowley Street is a beautiful set-piece, an example of architecture as sophisticated scenography. Lutyens, a contemporary of Fields, even had a term for it – Wrenaissance – which punningly captured the sense of rediscovering a previous era. But the work also updated Wren and the Queen Anne period, adding a sense of Georgian discipline to the composition of elevations as well as the pragmatism of developing streets and squares to make a city.

If we traced a timeline we would see that what we call neo-Geo today is a revival of the neo-Georgian architecture of the inter- and immediate post-war years in the UK, which itself is a revival of the Queen Anne Revival architecture of the Edwardian period, which

FIG. 5 Cowley Street, London, designed by Horace Field.

is a revival of the architecture of the very early eighteenth century practised by Wren, which was in turn highly influenced by the architecture of the Italian Renaissance, which was predicated on a return to the principles of building in ancient Rome. There is a sense of forward motion here, of one style shifting to another. But there is also a sense of consciously returning to the styles of previous eras. This is a story of continual revivals, evolutions of old ideas that recur in different forms at different times.

This is not an argument for the naturalisation or inevitability of such an architecture. But it is perhaps an argument against the idea of linear progression and the tendency to regard architectural history as a series of unique stylistic periods. And there is surely something interesting and enjoyable about buildings that confound expectations of when they were built and play games with the history of architecture. In his book *The Edwardians and Their Houses*, Timothy Brittain-Catlin points out that the early years of the twentieth century were a period of stylistic innovation, and one of the principal innovations was the self-conscious manipulation of historical elements. This stylistic eclecticism extended to a happy disassociation between interior and exterior. Houses drawing on rustic cottages or Elizabethan manors, for example, might often have neo-classical interiors or contain hints of art deco or even the modernism to come.

To conclude this section on stylistic returns, we will look briefly at the work of an architect who spent his career trying to revive the classical tradition. Raymond Erith was a classical architect in a modernist era. He started his career before the Second World War, designing an exquisite neo-Georgian house in Dedham in Essex called Great House. After the war, he continued to plough a lonely furrow, but his practice grew and he designed buildings for Queen's College, Oxford and oversaw the refurbishment of numbers 10 and 11 Downing Street. Erith's work was not just about revivalism: he developed unique and innovative ways to use the classical style. This was not the only paradox of his work. He would often deliberately blur the provenance of his buildings, sometimes making them appear older than they were, as if he had merely added to a genuinely historic piece of architecture. For Erith, the idea of expressing the age in which he was working was simply not important.

Style and Signature

So far, we have looked at style in general terms, as a way of designing that includes the work of different architects. But style can be seen as something highly individual, a kind of personal signature. The work of the Edwardian architect and designer Charles Voysey (fig. 6) is an interesting place to start such a conversation, not least because it reflects a tension between personal and more general ambitions. Voysey's work was relatively austere, an architecture reduced to essential qualities. Almost invariably finished in white, 'rough-cast' render, Voysey's houses relied on a refined sense of composition and proportion for their quality. They didn't do anything particularly spectacular, but they were consistently very, very good. By taking out much that he considered superfluous and by sticking rigidly to what he deemed to be a logical and unflamboyant set of principles, Voysey succeeded in developing a highly distinctive and personal style. Voysey houses are unmistakable. They almost all look the same: white walls, Westmorland slate roofs, leaded casement windows and an asymmetrical combination of gables, hips and chimneys.

Voysey used an obsessive repertoire of small details, too: red clay tiles to form the drips over his windows, wide, round-headed front doors, painted metal gutters and heart motifs. Heart motifs are everywhere in Voysey's designs: they appear in wrought-iron door hinges, carved into bedsteads, in the handles of his cutlery and in the oak newel posts of his staircases. Heart shapes were such an overwhelming feature of his work that when the novelist H.G. Wells commissioned Voysey to design his house, he played a subtle game of subversion. Wells was an inveterate gambler and a demon card player. Spades were his lucky suit, so he insisted that Voysey's hearts were flipped upside down to make spades. The house – built in Sandgate on the edge of Folkestone on the Kent coast – was named Spade House, enshrining Wells's strange act of sly homage.

Voysey's style – as unique and individual as it was – also became one of the most copied. There are derivations of Voysey's architecture all across the UK. We could say that Voysey inadvertently invented suburbia, or at least a certain kind of suburbia. Miniature Voysey houses form the backbone of the suburban expansions of the 1920s and 1930s. Voysey started the process himself, building Orchards – his own house – out on the fringes of London, connected to the city by the Metropolitan train line. Today the house is surrounded by the inter-war suburbia that it presaged, its highly refined and reduced version of historic domestic styles proving the perfect precedent for thousands of new homeowners.

FIG. 6 The Homestead, Frinton, Essex, designed by Charles Voysey.

There are a number of paradoxes to Voysey's work. The first is that a style so singular and individual could become so popular and widespread. Another is that the specificity of Voysey's work – his careful and highly considered choices of materials and elements – also became emblematic of a growing uniformity. Voysey's unwavering commitment to his own style was also his downfall. Having been an enormously popular architect who had defined an era and a style, he failed to move with the times or change his approach when it became unfashionable. Voysey ended his career with virtually no work, an architect out of time. His style was a victim of its own success. It had outgrown him and headed out into the world to populate a thousand arterial roads and suburban expansions. At the same time, the architectural world had moved on, embracing either a more extreme modernism for which Voysey had no time or a return to the familiarities of neo-Geo for which he had no stomach.

Zaha Hadid – the Ultimate Starchitect

Instances of individual style, of architects who irrefutably possess a personal signature, are rare. Zaha Hadid is one who did. Hadid was born in Baghdad and trained at the Architectural Association in London in the late 1970s and early 1980s. Hadid's final year of studying architecture had been marked by a period of illness, which she has described in interviews as a turning point during which she began to paint large, acrylic representations of her designs. These paintings became a method through which she developed a highly individual style.

On graduating she worked for her former tutor Rem Koolhaas and his influential practice, the Office for Metropolitan Architecture, or OMA. At first, her work appeared closely modelled on his, which in turn had developed out of an appropriation of early modernist architecture, including the work of the Russian Constructivists.

Hadid's final year of studying architecture had been marked by a period of illness which she has described in interviews as a turning point during which she began to paint large, acrylic representations of her designs. These paintings became a method through which she developed a highly individual style. Following her time working for Koolhaas she entered an international design competition for a building called the Peak (fig. 7), in Hong Kong. Hadid won the competition, and her drawings and paintings of the Peak came to define her career in spectacular style. She became almost instantly famous. The paintings – large, dramatic perspectives of her buildings – also became her architecture. Through them she could start to bend walls and explode plans. Surfaces became highly reflective or eerily transparent. Her jagged and fractured forms appeared to have floated in from somewhere else entirely and then stopped, momentarily, in space to form less a building than an assembly of forms that could – conceivably – become inhabited by people.

FIG. 7 The Peak, Hong Kong, painting by Zaha Hadid.

The paintings – which still drew on Constructivism and retained elements of a more conventional modernist architecture – made Hadid's career. Their formal power and distinctive voice exploded across the world of architecture. It helped that Hadid – unlike many architects – remained enigmatically disinclined to explain them. Seemingly, she had little in the way of a theory or explanation, which – in an architectural world of verbose theorising and incomprehensible essays – was a sort of relief in itself. Hadid could talk intelligently and authoritatively about many things, but her architecture seemed to come in some indefinable way from her own life force.

Hadid defined a style, a personal style that was based on an almost bodily relationship between her and her architecture. Her expansive paintings are an extension of her personality, a flamboyant gesture that could never find expression in tightly wound line drawings or architectural details. It was as if Hadid had to burst out of some confinement of normal representation in order to find her own architecture. One could define it to some extent: buildings made up of fragmented, crystalline forms caught during wilful and improbable acts of balance and implied movement. And it was unique, partly because it was very hard to copy or to do it remotely as well as Hadid.

Architecture is not generally an individual act. Despite the history of architecture appearing as a history of names, of singular achievements by individual authors, it is a collaborative activity. Buildings are big and expensive, and they are designed and realised by teams rather than individual geniuses. Even architectural drawings are the products of lots of people. It is rare – impossible, almost – for a single person to make all the drawings required for a construction project. And so architectural drawings proceed by conventions, ones that lots of people can contribute to and even more can interpret and read and translate into buildings.

Hadid's drawings changed that. They are not entirely exceptional. Many architects have developed singular and identifiable styles of drawing. But what makes Hadid different is the degree to which her style of architecture is personal, and its representation based on her own hand. The style of her architecture is an extension of the style of her drawings in a way that is highly unusual. Lots of architects have made significant individual stylistic leaps, but Hadid's appears the most personal and therefore inscrutable.

For a long time, it was assumed that her enigmatic and explosive drawings were essentially unbuildable. But she did eventually build, and her designs started to appear around the world as inhabited forms made of concrete and glass and steel and seemingly even keeping the rain out. Her office grew to become a large, global enterprise producing designs for airports and offices and art galleries. At that point something odd happened. Hadid's architecture moved away from her own signature. It became something that emerged from collective endeavour, subject to the influence of others.

Deconstructing Style

Despite its wilful individuality, Hadid's work was sometimes brought under the umbrella of a wider, stylistic genre: deconstruction. During the 1980s the influence of the French philosopher Jacques Derrida became significant in architecture. Derrida was credited with developing a branch of philosophy known as deconstruction, which concerned itself with the unpacking of many of the assumptions of Western thought. The new architectural style that adopted the name might have been rather simplistic in its interpretation of deconstruction's tenets – buildings that looked as if they were literally being deconstructed; spiky, explosive forms; and unstable-looking structures – but Derrida nevertheless became, unwittingly though not entirely unwillingly, its author.

This stylistic moment was inaugurated in the *Deconstructivist Architecture* exhibition at New York's Museum of Modern Art

(MoMA) in 1988. The exhibition was curated by Mark Wigley, a young architectural theorist, and Philip Johnson, New York's ageing but influential architect and kingmaker in residence. Johnson had co-curated the hugely influential *Modern Architecture: International Exhibition* at MoMA with Henry-Russell Hitchcock in 1932 and the *Deconstructivist Architecture* exhibition was a self-conscious, end-of-career attempt at another era-defining moment.

Zaha Hadid's work never quite fitted in, not least because she was uninterested in garnishing her designs with the kind of philosophical positioning that the style seemingly required. But other architects were happy to do so. The New York-based architect Peter Eisenman had already developed a successful career designing impossibly complex houses which leant heavily on the linguistic theories of Noam Chomsky.

Eisenman was in many ways the inverse of Hadid. He wrote extensively and in elliptical and opaque ways about his architecture, and was at pains to develop a theory that distanced it from mark-making and authorial tics. Rather than naming the houses he designed after their owners, he numbered them as if they were experiments to be recorded. And he described the process of their design as if they were the product of a series of objective, if strange, procedures. Eisenman's early series of houses came to a kind of perverse conclusion with House VI, a weekend home built in Cornwall, Connecticut in 1975. Eisenman's method involved a complex overlaying of grids, lines, columns and spaces during which he added and subtracted elements as if they were undergoing a mathematical realignment. The resulting house was full of perverse and surreal moments: a column that landed in the middle of the dining room, an upside-down staircase and a hole in the floor that meant the bed had to be cut in two. Later, Eisenman became an acolyte and an enthusiast of Derrida, and the two even collaborated on a project. Eisenman produced his own deconstructivist texts and explanations of his work, which attempted – or so he claimed – to undermine the history of Western architecture. Deconstructivism was a style at war with architecture, an approach that wanted to upend as many assumptions as possible. It was not a personal style – though there were common elements to it, used by different architects – but it became a stylistic moment, an intersection of fashionable concerns and contemporary theories.

This chapter has not been an exhaustive attempt to cover the A–Z of architectural styles. Instead, we have focused on different ways in which style manifests itself. We have looked at buildings – Homewood and the Sainsbury Wing – that combine several different styles together. We have looked at a recurring style – neo-Georgian – that returns again and again in different guises. We have looked at the supposed non-style of high-tech and the extreme style of deconstructivism. We have talked about style as zeitgeist and style as something that persists over time. We have looked at the idea of personal style through the vastly different work of Charles Voysey and Zaha Hadid. And we have considered style as a form of communication employed by architects to tell us what a building is trying to do or to say something about its role. We can see style as a way in.

CHAPTER 2

Composition

How do architects compose buildings? Painters compose paintings. Musicians compose music. And architects compose buildings. That seems simple enough. But buildings can be large and complex things. They can also contain lots of elements that while necessary are not especially desirable: toilets and kitchens and bin stores and garages and plumbing and electrical wiring and all sorts of other things that we might not consider when assessing their aesthetic merits. Are these composed, too? All these things need to work, and much of that working is really about function rather than artistic composition. There is a lack of purity to architecture, a sense that it is negotiating so much stuff that the art of composition becomes compromised by necessity, practicality and legislation and myriad other competing pressures.

Nevertheless, architects compose buildings. So how do they do this? Are there abstract rules that govern it, such as grids or mathematical ratios? Are there shapes that buildings are meant to fit into, and are these historically derived, based on past precedents? Or do architects start from scratch each time? Do buildings simply accumulate elements until all the required functions have been accommodated and nothing forgotten? How do architects even start this process?

Some buildings might appear to us as complete compositions, objects designed with an overall aesthetic aim in mind, such as a classical country house or a modernist skyscraper. But others come across as complex accumulations of parts, their ordering system – if they have one – more opaque and harder to discern. Symmetry and repetition suggest a rigorous compositional order. But asymmetrical or irregularly arranged buildings can be the result of careful composition, too.

If buildings are composed, it is in ways that are not necessarily always perceptible or visually legible. And we experience the various parts of an architectural composition in different ways, some visual and some in ways that are a mix of senses: touch, sound, smell. There is something else, too, which is that quite often when we look at or use buildings we are distracted. They are experienced in the compromise of rushing to work, or meeting someone, or going for a job interview or buying the week's shopping.

While we might not notice a piece of music or a painting in our everyday lives, often we have deliberately chosen to look at or listen to them. There is very little chance of missing a play in the heat of the moment. It is usually something we have chosen very deliberately to go to the theatre to watch, and while doing so we will give it our undivided attention. Architecture, though, is something that is part of the background of our lives and therefore we often miss it. Sometimes we visit buildings for their own sake: castles, stately homes, beautiful one-off houses, maybe even a particularly spectacular new building which becomes a destination. And when we do this, we afford them the careful attention and concentration that we give to art. But mostly we don't, and so the composition of buildings is both something we notice and something that we learn to navigate without necessarily giving it much thought.

Drawing and Architecture

One obvious way to describe what architects do when they compose buildings is to say that they make drawings. Drawings are not buildings, but they describe them in all sorts of ways. Architectural composition is both two- and three-dimensional: it involves the composition of drawings, but it also involves the relationship of rooms and elements and objects to each other, the relationship of surfaces to volumes and structure to space. Although composing architecture involves forms of representation – drawings, mostly, but also models, paintings, collages etc. – it is not itself a representational art. And nor is it reducible to the method used to represent it. Architecture is not the same as drawing, although we use drawings to make architecture.

The role of the architect or the designer involves a distance that is not always present in other art forms. We are used to contemporary artists not necessarily always making their own work; sometimes it is too large for that, and sometimes it might be because they are using industrial processes or – in, say, Marcel Duchamp's case – not actually making anything but simply taking an object that exists already and placing it in a gallery. But for the main part, art involves the artist working directly on the artwork itself. They might make preliminary sketches or maquettes, but at some point, the work involves the physical act of its own creation.

Architects – for the most part – do not build buildings. They work on drawings and models and rely on others, usually complex teams of builders and craftspeople, to make architecture. Composing a building is a movement, or a series of movements, between representation and building – from a largely two-dimensional mode of composition to a three-dimensional outcome. Composing buildings involves working at a scale – the scale of a drawing or a model – vastly different from that of a building. And it therefore involves a process of abstraction, of thinking about objects and spaces and materials in ways that are not actually present on the drawing but are represented by symbols or drawing conventions. It also involves composing objects that are sometimes very large and often very complex and unlikely ever to be experienced with the totality or the overview that the architect has when designing them.

Despite this, composition is governed by a dense interplay of criteria: artistic, practical, technical, legal and stylistic. What do

I mean by this? Well, all sorts of things happen in buildings and all sorts of requirements need to be taken care of. Resolving these into something that works across all the aspects of a building is a complex operation. Multiple types of drawings are used to do this. A building's plan – a horizontal slice through it – needs to align with its section – a vertical slice through it – and both need to work in tandem with its elevations – a vertical slice taken beyond the building looking straight at it.

Architects move between scales and modes of projection, from elevations to plans to elevations to details and back again, shuttling between these elements, sometimes unsuccessfully and never without complications, compromises and occasional crises. Composition, then, is both a discrete operation – like drawing a picture – and something which links that picture to the way buildings are built, what we do in them, the rules and regulations that govern their planning, the logics of their structure and, perhaps most mysteriously, what the architect wants to achieve artistically. Composition in architecture thus involves a lot of perhaps competing demands: aesthetic, practical, structural, legal, economic and myriad others. I am not trying to mythologise it, or make it sound more heroic than it is. The complexity of resolving these issues is also what makes it so satisfying to get right.

But how do we unpack these actions and tensions a little more and shed some light on what things govern a building's composition? To do this we might need to look at some of the individual modes of projection, the different types of drawings that architects use and the parts of the buildings they influence the most.

Elevations

Perhaps the most obvious way to talk about the composition of architecture is to look at elevations and the play and positioning of windows, walls and doors on a façade. We are more used to thinking of composition as a two-dimensional affair – through painting and image-making – and this is as close to that as architecture gets. It is also perhaps the most obvious way to assess style and assign some overall idea of what any particular building might want to say or communicate about itself.

Paintings might represent three dimensions but they themselves are flat and two-dimensional. Elevations aren't two-dimensional – at least not in terms of how we experience them in real life – but their relative flatness can be enough to equate them with the visual logic of a picture. They are the part of architecture that gets closest to a single, flat image and where visual, compositional relationships are most evident. Elevations follow rules of composition that relate to proportions and styles – or their rejection – and they also form the intersection of this visual order with the spatial order of a building: that is, there is a relationship between the internal spaces of a building and the way that these are expressed on the outside, on the elevation.

The Palazzo Rucellai (fig. 8) was designed in Florence in the 1440s by Leon Battista Alberti. The quintessential Renaissance man, Alberti began as a writer and linguist before shifting his interest to architecture. He studied the ancient ruins of Roman and Greek buildings and wrote his *Ten Books on Architecture*, the first consistent theory of classical architectural orders since Vitruvius in the Roman period. The Palazzo Rucellai was an attempt to put his theories of classical composition into physical form.

Its elevation is a highly sophisticated mapping of the classical orders derived from Roman buildings such as the Colosseum in Rome onto a fifteenth-century urban house, or palazzo in Florence. The main street elevation is split into three horizontal layers. Each layer is divided by a projecting cornice moulding, and each has its own order of classically derived pilasters – flat, non-structural columns – that form a vertical rhythm across the façade. The proportions of the columns – based on measurements of Roman architecture – dictate the heights of the internal floors and the size of the windows in between. It is a highly precise game, one where each part is locked into an overall system of proportion so that the whole has the complexity of a mathematical puzzle. As a design it proved almost too perfect, and the subsequent evolution of the Renaissance palazzo moved towards a freer and less demanding method of composition.

Alberti's work introduces the idea of perfection, a principle that elevations follow rules of scale, order, proportion and rhythm. His theory offers objective principles of achieving visual harmony and balance. What happens, though, if a building can't do this, if the circumstances of its design don't allow for such rigour? What happens if it falls short of perfection, allowing practical demands such as the need to accommodate an extra window or a second doorway or a taller chimney to mess with the rules?

FIG. 8 Palazzo Rucellai, Florence, designed by Leon Battista Alberti.

We have already been introduced to the work of Robert Venturi and Denise Scott Brown (VSBA) in the opening chapter, when we discussed their design for the Sainsbury Wing extension to the National Gallery. Their work represents a rich and rewarding exploration of the way that architecture must negotiate both ideal and pragmatic impulses. This negotiation is often most apparent in the elevations of their buildings, which combine several orders or drivers in compositions of great subtlety and tension.

In 1966, Robert Venturi published a book called *Complexity and Contradiction in Architecture* in which he elaborated a theory of architecture that grew out of the competing demands facing the architect. Venturi argued for an architecture that admitted to conflict and – in a sense – made meaning out of compromise. Instead of Alberti's purity and perfection, Venturi argued for a plurality of sources and an enjoyment of what he termed contradiction: the points at which competing demands might become part of the composition of a building. His architecture – designed with a variety of collaborative partners but for the longest period with Scott Brown, his wife – are studiedly imperfect. In Venturi's terms, they are complex and contradictory.

Take Fire Station Number 4 (fig. 9), a seemingly simple municipal building realised in the town of Columbus, Indiana in 1966, the same year as the publication of Venturi's enormously influential book. Fire Station Number 4 is a relatively straightforward composition in many ways: a medium-sized shed offering a garage for the fire trucks. But this is also a building that wants to be a piece of architecture, an elegant and well-proportioned shed with some of the qualities of a classical building. It is a shed that has read Alberti's *Ten Books of Architecture*.

Much of the tension between this aspiration and the actual demands of its functional needs is played out on the front, street-facing elevation. This has the quality of a billboard, a deliberately simple, flat façade. It is also taller than the shed behind it in order

FIG. 9   Fire Station Number 4, Columbus, Indiana, designed by VSBA.

to clearly delineate that this is the entrance façade, rather in the manner of a stage set. The façade also has a tower, located centrally and symmetrically like the bell tower of a church. Most of the front elevation is in white brick, but this material doesn't quite cover the entire surface, with the 'leftover' parts in plain red brick.

The white brick describes a perfect elevation rather than the actual one. Dictated by clear, practical demands, including the size and number of fire trucks required, the elevation is – in VSBA's terms – slightly too wide and slightly too flat. These imperfect proportions are masked by the areas of white brick. It is as if they have drawn the proportions of the buildings that they would have *liked* to have designed onto the one they have had to design. There is a sleight of hand here, because ultimately it is the tension between the aspiration to perfection and the compromised reality that is important. VSBA's particular contribution is to formulate a theory of architecture based on the impossibility of a theory of architecture to anticipate all events. As a result, beauty comes with an added poignancy, that of it not being quite perfect.

VSBA's usefulness in a conversation about composition is that they formulated a clear position that recognises imperfection and allows us to see it as a virtue. What Venturi refers to in his book as 'messy vitality' is really the stuff of life getting in the way of architecture, a problem that he turns into a value. Composition – in both plan and elevation – is a way to communicate this messy vitality.

Plans

A pattern of windows across a façade – or even an absence of windows – is never just that. It occurs in plan and section too, where its compositional qualities can be very different and where it intersects with experience, with the amount of light that window brings in, with the view that it frames or the intrusion into a neighbour's privacy that it avoids. These adjustments are governed by a sort of common sense – one places the window for a bathroom high in the room, say, or a door in a wall to allow an adequate area for it to swing open – but they are part of a wider set of principles that architects subscribe to in ways that are sometimes explicit and deliberate and sometimes implicit and habitual.

Unlike elevations, we don't see plans. Plans are experienced, but only partially – we rarely inhabit all of a building and certainly not at the same time. Even in buildings we use or visit a lot, some parts remain unknown, out of reach or simply not relevant. And we see and use different bits every time, so we experience plans in non-linear and non-sequential ways. Despite this, plans are composed and – like elevations – aspects of their composition are visual and aesthetic: that is, plans have an obligation to work, to accommodate and find space for all the things we need in a building, but they also strive to be aesthetic compositions *in their own right*. Plans can be beautiful. They can be elegant and refined in ways that we never experience except through an appreciation of them as drawings. This might seem odd. Why bother? Is this just architecture for architects, a sort of private pleasure? Maybe, but perhaps we would understand a little more about the impulse to draw a perfect plan if we looked at a building that has one.

Perfect Composition

A good place to start looking for perfection in architectural planning is the work of the Italian Renaissance architect Andrea Palladio, specifically the series of villas he designed and built in the Veneto – the area around the city of Venice – during the sixteenth century. These villas achieve a form of compositional perfection, a sublime reconciliation of practical and artistic ambitions that renders them hugely significant in the history of architecture.

Mostly, the villas were built for wealthy Venetian families as their country residences. But they were also sometimes working buildings, farms that included outbuildings, barns and grain stores. Their use was more complex than their outward form would suggest. Villa Almerico Capra (also known as Villa Rotonda; fig. 10) is the best-known and certainly the most celebrated example. The plan is perfectly symmetrical, an essay in bilateral symmetry where each of the building's four sides is identical.

Each elevation has a central portico – a triangular pediment supported by six Ionic columns – through which one enters the villa. The raised ground floor is reached by a grand, external flight of steps that leads up to this portico. We are used to houses having backs and fronts and for these to be differentiated in terms of impor-tance and hierarchy. The plan of the Villa Rotonda has four fronts and no back. The plan of the house is a cross, a perfect square with four projecting staircases. At the centre of the square is a perfect circle. In section, this circle forms a large, double-height hallway surmounted by a shallow dome.

Around the circular space, spaces are arranged in a grid of interconnected rooms. You can walk around this house in a circle, moving from one room to the next in sequence. There are no corridors, no dead spaces, no awkward moments and seemingly no mistakes. The rooms have no specific functions, either. You could put a bed in one and a dining table in another, and you could swap them around another day, and it wouldn't much matter. They are not shaped to their function, and they don't vary in size that much, either. They are simply spaces, rooms, ready for inhabitation.

The Villa Rotonda appears both removed from everyday reality and, at the same time, thoroughly grounded in it. Living here

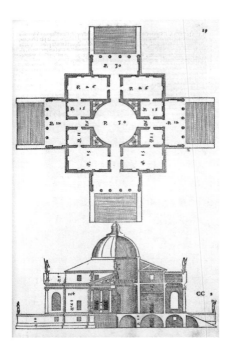

FIG. 10 Plan of the Villa Rotonda, Vicenza, designed by Andrea Palladio.

appears from our vantage point to be a pure experience, an ideal. Palladio has seemingly raised domestic life to an extraordinary level of abstract perfection. It is not quite as pure as it might seem at first, of course. The more prosaic functions of the house – cooking and storage and the inevitable servants' quarters – are located below the principal, raised ground floor in a semi-basement level. This distribution – lower ground-floor servant spaces with a piano nobile, or raised ground floor, above – occurs in almost all of Palladio's country villas. The upper floor is for bedrooms and sometimes – improbably – for storing grain, which acted usefully as a form of insulation.

The villas achieve a level of almost icy perfection. Somehow the messy contingencies of life have been ordered into something that speaks of a composed, methodically coordinated order. Windows are where they need to be both in plan and in elevation because the relationship between the plan and the form of the building is inseparable. The same organising intelligence means that compositionally this is a building that brooks no argument, admits no doubt. It is an object of fearsome clarity and compositional power.

Villa Rotonda is the most perfect, the most pristine and the most extreme of Palladio's houses. It represents symmetry and order taken to an almost impossible level, where the principle of each identical façade and the symmetry of its plan admits no compromise or imperfection. It is a temple in the landscape, approached across the surrounding fields like a citadel. Palladio's other houses are all derivations of this idea, their plans a pattern book of subtle variations and refinements.

English Palladianism

Like Alberti before him, Palladio produced a comprehensive theoretical account of his work. His *Four Books on Architecture* became hugely influential in the development of Western architecture, disseminating an approach that became truly international. Palladio's work exerted a particularly strong influence on the development of architecture in the UK, where it became the dominant stye during the first half of the eighteenth century. Country houses, civic buildings, theatres and even agricultural buildings became Palladian in style.

But in their translation from practical residences for sixteenth-century Italian farmers to the country estates of wealthy Georgians, Palladio's principles underwent a subtle transformation that tells us something interesting about how plans intersect with people. We have already seen that Palladio's country villas were composed as a series of interconnected rooms. Spaces were not ascribed uses in quite the way that we are used to today. Ideas around privacy and separation were different, too. To get to a room in a Palladian house one travels through several other rooms first. They are like beads on a string, one space after another.

When Palladianism was imported to the UK – by proselytisers such as Colen Campbell and Lord Burlington – something interesting happened to it. The lack of privacy and social hierarchy of Palladio's grids of rooms was unacceptable to a society that depended on social segregation. There was simply not enough privacy in a Palladian plan, no way to enforce separations of gender, age and class in the way that the evolving British society thought necessary. So Palladio's perfect plans started to grow corridors and secondary means of circulation, and these began to require additions and extensions to the plan. The result was a huge compromise. The beauty and brilliance of Palladio's compositions came up sharply against the practical and psychological complexities of eighteenth-century English society. An approach to the composition of buildings based on the social conventions of one society needed to be adapted to meet those of another.

The relationship between social space and architectural space is an acute one: a sort of battleground between different impulses. But an accommodation to social rituals does not have to result in architectural compromise. It might in fact be an agent of how to achieve a kind of compositional perfection.

The Georgian Town House

If Palladio had to be updated to meet the demands of eighteenth-century Britain, other architects took those same demands and developed an architecture specifically for it. Georgian society evolved new forms of domestic architecture that fitted its customs much more closely. In his book *Georgian Architecture in London*, the historian and critic Sir John Summerson describes the domestic plans of Robert Adam as the pinnacle of that period's architectural compositional attainment.

The Georgian town house was a product of various forces. Most obviously it related to the development model of Georgian cities, where areas were laid out according to a pattern of streets and squares with individual plots developed by different builders. The plots and the solution were largely consistent over a long period of time, consisting of four- or five-storey buildings joined together as terraces. Ground-floor entrances led to a stairway to the principal floor – or piano nobile – which contained the main rooms for entertaining. Above these were bedrooms and servants' quarters. Materials – brick walls, timber floors and slate roofs – were also consistent.

The interior demands were based on the formal requirements of eighteenth- and early nineteenth-century social life, so that the Georgian house was primarily organised around the rituals of entertaining and the separation of those doing the entertaining (the family) from those enabling it (their servants). Adam's achievement was to reconcile these multiple requirements into a more sophisticated composition than any architect before him. The formal and processional requirements of the interior – a series of rooms laid out to contain and choreograph guests – reaches a peak of perfection within the material, structural and economic envelope in which the houses were held. His houses can be seen as a highly complex composition in which practical demands and social ceremony are aesthetically resolved to an extraordinarily high degree.

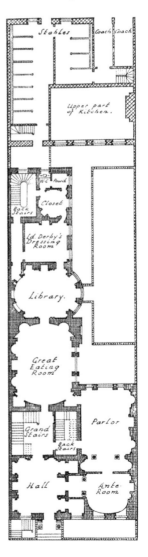

The interior of an Adam house (fig. 11) – at least, the parts of the interior that he and his clients were most concerned with – is a procession, a journey from the entrance through to reception rooms and then on to retiring or music rooms. The chronology of Georgian domestic entertaining results in a plan based on a promenade, a sequence interrupted by moments of talking, eating and repose.

Robert Adam was not working alone but within an active tradition and a highly structured social milieu. His buildings reflected and refined a set of existing and emerging compositional rules within what might be called the logic of the development industry of his day. All buildings must do this to some degree. The most ordinary house is composed to meet various forms of expectation in terms of lifestyle, taste, expense, aspiration etc. One could say that buildings are an aggregation of those issues and others, an accumulation of often competing demands. The resolution of these demands is one of the challenges of architectural composition.

FIG. 11 Plan of Derby House, London, designed by Robert Adam.

The design of the Georgian town house – of which Adam was a refined and leading exponent – was governed, then, by three main things: the economic logic of parcels of land developed within established urban conditions; the social structure and habits of the families who lived in them; and an increasingly regulated construction industry. If the first aspect dictated the overall volume of the house and the second its internal organisation, the final element was the pattern book of columns, decorative doorcases and ornamental mouldings that were applied to the houses like the cutlery laid out on the dinner tables within. An intersection of craftspeople, carpenters, builders and developers allowed the construction and embellishment of these houses in a highly efficient manner.

This was a form of composition governed and held in check by social and economic protocols. It is why Georgian houses largely look the same up and down the country: the same materials, windows, doors and methods of composition. Georgian architecture swept away difference and vernacular nuance in favour of a stylish and fashionable idiom propelled by an economy increasingly able to move people and materials around, regardless of location or local tradition. The Georgians 'Georgianified' existing buildings when they weren't building new ones, so that small cottages or farmhouses took on the same appearance. This resulted in strange anomalies including unsymmetrical or eccentric façades attempting to regularise highly irregular buildings, and the dislocation between the composition of elevations and the interiors they enclosed.

The Georgian house and its interior – as well as, of course, its social structures – forms the basis and background for many of Jane Austen's novels. There is even a joke about domestic architecture in *Emma* regarding the ubiquity of the Georgian house plan. When the character Mrs Elton extols the novelty of the layout of her cousin's new house, the contemporary reader would have recognised the unintended humour. There was very, very little novelty in the layout of the Georgian house – almost none, in fact. They were all the same.

This uniformity – almost a form of mass production – was in sharp and obvious contrast to what came after it in the UK. This was a return to the wilful eccentricity and asymmetrical individuality of the Gothic ushered in by the work of Augustus Pugin.

One as Many

Augustus Pugin's own house, the Grange, overlooks the English Channel in the town of Ramsgate. It is part of a composition of buildings that includes his own private chapel – St Augustine's – along with others added by his architect son Edward after his death. The house itself breaks decisively with classical Georgian models in ways that are stylistic and spatial. While the Georgian house offered a familiar, ubiquitous plan of hallway and receptions rooms, Pugin's Grange employs a pinwheel formation with rooms orbiting a central hall. Inside, the house is a riot of pattern, colour and decoration: wallpaper enlivened with Latin slogans, banisters carved with symbols, all manner of stained glass and a picturesque tower that winds up through the house to pop out above the roofline to give a bracing view of the sea.

Pugin lived here with his wife and thirteen children, a maelstrom of manic overwork, religious observance and intense proselytising. The house is a manifesto and a polemic. It is a frantic composition where rooms are expressed as individual components within the plan, differently sized and each expressed on the exterior. The visual propriety of Georgian architecture, which squeezed the disparate elements of the whole into a highly regulated container, is here shaken up and thrown around. Pugin smashes open the respectable container. Windows sit not in carefully contained alignment, but where he wants them to go. They vary in size and style. There are battlements, bays, tall towers and pointed gables. It may look relatively normal to us now, accustomed as we are to its style and history, but it was once a little revolution.

Pugin is the anti-Adam. All that limpid and elegant ornament is replaced by intense, blood-red letters and dense foliage. The Grange seems intentionally to burst out of the confines of the Georgian compositional box, announcing its elements and the life within with exaggerated expression. Pugin was a pious and intensely religious man. It would be wrong to interpret his house as some kind of paean to excess. Its exterior materials and forms appear familiar to us now from Victorian rectories and parsonages the country over. But compositionally we are in a different world, one without the classical orders, without symmetry or proportional hierarchies, and one where rooms are not subordinate to an overall form but expressed as volumes in their own right.

So here we have a very different conception of how a house is composed. It is not as if Pugin's Grange is uncomposed – its freedom is to some extent an illusion. Its architect has carefully pushed and pulled the volumes to form a composition that is carefully balanced but also achieves a quality of movement and dynamism. But obvious disciplines and confining forms of classical composition have been abandoned. The one has become many.

Many as One

If Pugin's Grange represents the fragmentation of one house into many, the house built by the Sri Lankan architect Geoffrey Bawa (fig. 12) is the opposite: a series of fragments collected together as one entity. The plan of Bawa's house is complex and additive: it feels like a series of rooms and spaces stuck together to fill the available space. At first no obvious order seems to exist. It is a collection of rooms rather than a clear composition. It has no obvious shape or order.

Bawa built his house over time, starting in 1958 and expanding to fill adjacent plots as they became available. What began as a single, modest bungalow in a backstreet of Colombo grew like an organic entity to absorb the sites of three other houses. Eventually Bawa designed and built for himself a formidably large house that occupied an entire city lot. There is no obvious distinction between house and garden, or public and private spaces. Instead, one room leads to another, sometimes separated by little courtyards that are themselves like outdoor rooms.

It is like a labyrinth, or a jigsaw puzzle, its interlocking shapes slotted together with a seemingly impenetrable organisational or circulation system. Some of the spaces contain furniture and water features, trees and other plants. Some even have cars in them – the parking space for Bawa's ostentatious Rolls Royce Silver Ghost

FIG. 12   33rd Lane, Colombo, designed by Geoffrey Bawa.

is included in his drawings. Though it looks ad hoc, the plan is carefully and artfully composed. Doors are lined up with other openings. Columns frame views. Light enters from unexpected, hidden sources that nonetheless make sense of certain spaces or lead the visitor towards others.

Bawa's house has little or no external character and formally it is hardly there at all. It is introverted and intense rather than extrovert and spectacular. It is not an object in space – like Palladio's Villa Rotonda – but a series of bounded spaces. It is like a warren, a house without an exterior. Its composition is the grid-like interconnection of spaces freed from the need to make elevations or external expression. It is an architecture of space, of rooms and activities. And it is a single storey in height. It has no stairs and no sectional complexity. It is, in a way, *all* plan.

Composing Types

Another way to think about the composition of buildings is to consider them in terms of types. Typology is the study of building as a taxonomy of types, forms of buildings that have responded to certain programmatic and functional requirements. Often this is not about specific functions so much as more general ones, or ones that relate to each other over time. An example of this would be the stoa, a building type that recurs through architectural history to accommodate functions where a long, repetitive series of spaces is useful. Examples of this include the market or arcade or even the high street, where individual units are lined up one after the other. The stoa responds to a need that transcends particular times or eras and can be found at different moments in architectural history.

The stoa is a compositional type, a form of building where the spatial organisation is to some degree a given, a kind of 'found object'. Typology is a study of how certain forms of building organisation persist over time. This is not a neutral argument, as it assumes or is prone to a bias around ideas of continuity and a sense that architecture is an evolutionary process. It is resistant to radical changes (what you could call new typologies), preferring to stress continuity over innovation.

Typology provides an idea of how buildings can be arranged but it is not in itself a complete composition. Instead, it emphasises the transcendence of type over stylistic, aesthetic or material shifts. In effect a stoa could be designed in many different styles, and it can be nuanced in many ways, though its basic form – a colonnade in front of a series of smaller spaces – remains the same.

So is typology the same as composition? Not entirely. Typology can be seen as an element of composition. It might provide a structural part of the composition or inform it in some way or form its basis. But composition is different, and importantly it implies change and the development of a layout that responds to a unique situation as much as a more general one.

As the Spanish architect Rafael Moneo writes: 'Composition is the tool by which the architect deals with the variety of programs offered by the new society.' It is worth breaking this comment down. First, 'program' in architectural terminology means use or function. A 'house' is a program, as is a 'cinema' or a 'supermarket'. Second, what does Moneo mean by the 'new society'? Well, here he is referring to an idea that architecture both reflects and gives form to new social ideas – that is, as we develop new activities such as new forms of medical practice or the home office, architecture responds with new types of buildings and spaces that can house these activities.

In his book *The Language of Post-Modern Architecture*, the critic and historian Charles Jencks took the German modernist architect Ludwig Mies van der Rohe to task for the supposed semantic confusion of his work. Writing specifically about the Illinois Institute of Technology campus, designed by Mies in 1952, Jencks suggested that a layman would find the architecture deeply confusing on a typological level. Jencks claimed that the university chapel is housed in a building that has the utilitarian appearance of a boiler room. Conversely, the actual boiler room, with its symmetrical form and large, centrally placed chimney, looks like a chapel. Jencks is of course being mildly facetious in this comparison and exaggerating for effect. Nonetheless, he has a point, which is to do with expectations of building form and composition that can be read at the level of type.

Another way of thinking about type is to use the word genre. Buildings have genres in the same way that books or films do. For romcoms, heist movies and the Western we could read arcades, banks and castles. There are basic assumptions and aspects of familiarity that ground each one in a kind of popular understanding of the form. We judge them – to some extent – on the way that they perform in relation to an established genre. Buildings communicate in this way too – conforming to type, you might say. We learn to navigate much of the built environment this way, through culturally specific tropes or norms of building organisation and composition driven by type.

Some buildings both conform to and destabilise such typologies, sticking to some conventions while flouting others. Sometimes this is deliberate. And some buildings make the combination of typologies part of the point. A good example of this is the work of twentieth-century British architect James Stirling, which can often look and feel like several very different buildings combined – not always comfortably – together. The plan of Stirling's Social Science Centre in Berlin, for instance, is like a mash-up of different buildings, each one representing a very specific type: cruciform church, stoa, tower and castle. It is as if several models of historic buildings had been thrown together, landing where they fell, and then been requisitioned for random new purposes.

Here, the connection of function to type has been severed so that the form of the building is no longer particularly related to its use.

The part that looks – at least from above – like a church is divided into offices in much the same way that the part that looks like a theatre is. And the forms are only legible at the level of an overall footprint. In terms of materials, style and sculptural expression, each element departs markedly from its reference point. Each part is in fact faced in the same pastel-coloured, striped render, like a set of different toys made from the same material. Stirling's point no doubt is that the forms have some lingering popular meaning but are no longer suitable for anything specific. The form of a church is useful only as a thing that we might vaguely recognise and thus make sense of, or, at least, drag from the recesses of our memories to provide some form of meaning.

Buildings have become generally more complex than historic typologies allow. It is hard to make contemporary buildings that simple or that legible. They have grown all sorts of other requirements. They are complex objects full of machines as well as people, no longer reducible to archetypes or simple, recognisable forms. It takes time and money to make architecture simpler, perversely enough.

Aldo Rossi: Composition and Memory

There are instances of architectural composition attempting to match the simplicity and clarity of paintings, of moments when art and architecture become closely intertwined in ways that shed light on the use of composition in both. And there are ways in which architecture is composed like painting, when it seeks a clarity of composition comparable to the classical villas of Palladio.

The work of the twentieth-century Italian architect Aldo Rossi is interesting in this respect because his buildings explore the idea of typology in a particularly rigorous way, and because he used painting to establish a series of compositional elements that are deployed almost regardless of programme. Rossi's work has been described as neo-rationalist, partly because it self-consciously refers to the rationalist architecture of the eighteenth and early nineteenth centuries, a period when classical archetypes were applied to the emerging industrial programmes of European cities.

Rossi took these archetypes and through his paintings invested them with a sense of melancholy and reflection. His paintings suggest a city made up of recurring elements – towers, monuments, arcades and temples – that are like the relics of a previous civilisation. Rossi's paintings have been compared to the work of the Italian surrealist Giorgio de Chirico, who also painted eerily empty city plazas and streets inhabited only by long shadows or a puff of smoke from a passing steam train.

Rossi appears to be saying that all we have is these remains. All we can do is try to reassemble them, mix them around and try to draw from their lingering metaphysical power. His paintings are populated by his own memories: huddles of small beach cabins, a single column from a long-lost building, quotes from his own previous work. Rossi's contention was that architecture doesn't need new forms. Any current building can be composed using the various archetypes that already exist and that have existed for several centuries.

Rossi's work is the opposite of a search for the new. It is based on the obsessive revisiting of things that already exist. His work involves an archaeology of architecture where typology is both an effective mechanism for making new buildings and a reflection on the city as a form of collective memory. Rossi combines not just archetypal fragments of buildings but memories, too.

Unlike de Chirico, Rossi was not only describing existing spaces but proposing new ones too. And his buildings retain a formal purity and power even as their programmes grew. Almost uniquely, Rossi's buildings have a simplicity and an archetypal character that belies the complexity of their briefs.

Rossi's compositions look almost childish in their simplicity. Buildings are made up of the sort of blocks that might be used in a toy city: cubes, triangles and spheres are added to simple blocks forming courtyards and long terraces, with punched-out, repetitive windows. His most famous building is the cemetery at Modena, in northern Italy, partially completed in 1971 (fig. 13). Here, simple shed-like forms run around a vast perimeter rectangle. They sit on thin concrete fin-like legs that cast long shadows in the Italian sun. In the centre is a red cubic volume punctured by many windows. The smallness of the windows and their repetitive nature obscures the scale, making the object both large and small at the same time, like a giant toy. It has very little detail.

The red cube is an ossuary, a space for human remains. No one lives there and the windows have no glass. It is an empty building – a house for the dead, in Rossi's own terms – and it is perhaps therefore the ultimate Rossian building. Freed from the need to make a fully functioning enclosure, his design reaches a level of singular power. His composition is more like that of a painting than a building: it obeys pictorial rules, seemingly largely untouched by practical need. In the Modena cemetery, Rossi managed to fuse the compositional clarity of painting with the complexity of architecture.

FIG. 13 Aerial perspective of San Cataldo Cemetery, Modena, designed by Aldo Rossi.

He created a picture and composed something that might be called pure building. It is architectural composition at its purest, simplest and most compelling.

Through this chapter we have looked at architectural composition in various ways: as a product of how architects draw, as a reflection of social organisation, as an assemblage of precedents and historic types and as a kind of body made up of individual objects. We have seen it conceived as something essentially flat and two-dimensional – plans, elevations and sections – that can be put together into a three-dimensional object and as something that starts with existing objects and types. We have discussed how it intersects with function and with architectural programme and how the compromises that this entails might in themselves give rise to architectural qualities.

The composition of buildings reflects many things, not all of which are readily understandable when we inhabit architecture. Both the size and the complexity of buildings can make their composition hard to grasp. But composition is the controlling device that holds architecture together. Although I have separated it from structure and from style in the chapters of this book, it really contains both. When I sit down to try to compose a building, myriad things come into play. I shuttle back and forth between them, and between drawings, models and sketches, and between aesthetic and functional demands, and between the detail and the whole. That is what composition is. Its outcome is both an object and something else. And that something else is called space.

CHAPTER 3

Space

O F all the words or aspects of architectural terminology, space is perhaps the obscurest. Architects use the term often, but what are they referring to? It is easier to describe what space *isn't* than what it is. It isn't the building itself. It isn't the walls, and it isn't the objects in a room. It's not light or colour or even temperature. So what is it?

Space is seemingly intangible, the one thing that is not actually there. It could be something to do with atmosphere – the 'feel' of a room, for example – but it is also used to describe a more general sense of how a building is laid out and composed. We have talked about composition in the previous chapter, so here we will focus more on the *result* of that composition, what we could call the spatial consequences of how buildings and rooms and objects are arranged.

It might not help that architects themselves use the term in different ways to mean different things. Sometimes space is employed simply as a unit of measure, such as the dimensions of a room. Architects will refer to the size of spaces, by which they simply mean how large a volume is. A spatial breakdown might in this case be a list of rooms and their dimensions. There's nothing particularly complex about this, and if it were the only way the term was used then this might be a short chapter.

But what happens when the qualities or character of a space itself need to be described? Rather than positioning spaces according to clear hierarchies, architects describe spatial characteristics that are more subjective. Sometimes a value is added to the basic unit of space, such as 'this is a rather beautiful space'. Describing a space as beautiful implies qualities that are not clearly measurable. Is it the space we are describing, or the walls of the room enclosing it? It is common to react to dramatic or beautiful spaces – the nave of a cathedral or the hallway of a grand house, for instance. This might be due to a combination of elements, something to do with the proportions of the room, the lavishness of the materials, the richness of the decoration or possibly even the view.

Problems set in when we move to less palpable value judgements. Describing the spatial sequence of a house, for instance, is clearly about the order and the arrangement of rooms but it is also something to do with the nature of that arrangement itself and the three-dimensional qualities that it might possess. We can talk of flowing space, open-plan space, cellular space or perhaps 'contained' space. These are all terms that describe how walls and doors and staircases are arranged, but they also describe the result of such things, the residual *outcome* of arranging them in particular ways.

This residue is also the part of buildings that we inhabit, the volume that we move around in as well as where we talk, work, cook, sleep, watch TV, wash, etc. So space is essential to an understanding of how we *use* architecture. Although it is an absence – the bit that we can't touch or look at or lean on – it is also the part of a building most useful to us. It is space that we occupy and use. It is *our* bit. So we can say that space describes something, even if we are not entirely sure yet what that something really is.

Leon Battista Alberti, the designer of the Palazzo Rucellai, wrote that 'the city is like a great house, and the house in its turn is a small city'. In this chapter, we will examine the qualities of space first through the house and then through the city. We will take the most familiar experience of space – the houses we inhabit – and zoom out from there to explore how space is experienced at larger scales. We will look at space as something contained within a house and at the house itself as something that exists within a wider space.

Solid Space

If space is conceived as an absence – the void between walls – what happens when we reverse that relationship? What results if we make space the solid, tangible thing and the walls enclosing it an absence? Might that tell us something about the nature of space itself? We might at least be able to *see* space, measure some of its qualities, touch it even.

The twentieth-century Italian architect Luigi Moretti used casting to understand the spatial layouts of different buildings. In an article written in 1951 for the Italian magazine *Spazio*, Moretti used photographs of cast models of the interiors of well-known buildings to distinguish between different kinds of space. He used examples ranging from the Renaissance – such as Michelangelo's San Giovanni chapel in Florence – to the relatively recent – such as Mies van der Rohe and Lilly Reich's Barcelona Pavilion, built in 1928–9.

In this inverted form the buildings are barely recognisable, more like skeletons than full bodies. One can guess the type of building – a church, for instance – but not necessarily the specific example. In this sense, the models define genres of space, different general rules that relate to different types of building. Moretti used the models to demonstrate differences in spatial configuration between these building types without the distractions of style or material getting in the way. We can see examples of space that is more or less compartmentalised, or flowing, space that is hierarchical and centralised or open-ended and informal. Moretti's casts are enigmatic and strange objects, and they undoubtedly reveal something new. But they are also quite alienating, literally turning our world inside out so that the space we inhabit becomes impenetrable and opaque too. In some senses, they make space more mysterious, not less.

Moretti's casts are models, too, so that we are seeing and touching space at a distance and a scale different from inhabiting a real building. The work of the English artist Rachel Whiteread uses the same technique as Moretti but at full scale. Whiteread is best known for her casts of otherwise intangible places: the gap between the underside of a chair and the floor, the narrow slots between books in a library and – in her most ambitious work – the interior of a typical London Victorian house. Her temporary 1993 artwork *House* (fig. 14) consisted of a cast of the interior of a three-storey house. The walls, roof, windows and doors no longer exist, and what's left is a lump of concrete approximating the interior volume of the absent house. No, not just approximating. It *is* the interior of the house. The outer edge of the concrete contains the imprint of the containing walls, an inverted cast of the doorways, fireplaces

FIG. 14   Rachel Whiteread, *House*, 1993. 193 Grove Road, London E3. Destroyed 1993.

and windows that are no longer there. Even the soot from around the chimney breast leaves its presence in the form of a blackening of the concrete casting at this point.

Whiteread's *House* is domestic space made physically manifest. It is literally a cast of the space that we formerly occupied, a solid room with invisible walls. What does *House* tell us about the nature of this space? Clearly, in making it Whiteread is drawing our attention to something that is overlooked, or ignored, perhaps because it surrounds us to such an extent that we are blind to it. Instead of describing space as a negative – the gap between things – Whiteread seems to suggest that space is *stuff.* It is something positive that shapes and holds us. Space is what we exist *in.*

House is the most ambitious piece in a series of casts of domestic spaces made by Whiteread over several years. A previous piece, called *Ghost,* involved the casting of a single room, for example. *Ghost* is a more enigmatic and revealing title than *House.* It captures the elusiveness of Whiteread's enterprise, the sense that she is a sort of detective on the hunt for something that has gone missing. Perhaps what Whiteread is doing in all these pieces is to try to catch a phantom, an elusive trace of something present but invisible.

The ghost in Whiteread's *House* is not the absent container but the thing inside it. She reverses the polarities, which allows us to understand what it is that we are inhabiting. In a sense, Whiteread's work achieves what architects often attempt to do, which is to make space the subject of architecture. In her work, objects – decoration, ornaments, the bits that occupy space – become secondary and less important. Architects often claim that buildings are about space, as if they are verbally doing what Whiteread does physically, removing the unnecessary baggage of ordinary life and allowing us to concentrate on the essence of something more important. The ineffability of space might here be an advantage, allowing a glimpse of the previously unknowable and ultimately profound quality of architecture.

Whiteread captures the space within an ordinary London home. Some of the power of her work relies on the familiarity of this as a source. The Victorian terrace is a type familiar to many of us, its layout relatively ubiquitous. We can 'read' Whiteread's piece partly because we recognise the traces of something familiar. In this sense her work is also about memory and familiarity. It is not purely about space, then, but what spaces mean to us. Whiteread's work is not analytical. She appears less interested in telling us what different kinds of space are than in tapping into our memories of familiar spaces. Her work is powerful and useful to us here in giving form to something that we noted at the outset as slippery and absent.

If Moretti's models and Whiteread's sculptures allow us to see something previously invisible, they also rely heavily on memory and prior knowledge. To understand them we need a solid working knowledge of the thing they are attempting to describe. What happens if the space is less familiar? What happens when an architect tries to do something new with space, something that undermines the sense of familiarity or recognition? If Whiteread's *House* helps us to understand the existing, familiar spaces of home, how do we start to characterise less familiar space? Rather than describing spaces that already exist, we need to ask another question: how do architects *design* spaces? And are these spaces palpably different from the ones that have existed before?

Radical Space

We could start to answer these questions by trying to understand if there are different kinds of 'space', different ways that this immaterial material can be sliced up or arranged or composed. Take, for example, the difference between an open-plan house and one with a more traditional arrangement of rooms. Whiteread's *House* is a cast of a very traditional spatial arrangement. Rooms – spaces – are discrete and cellular. They are separated by doors and by corridors, which are themselves distinct kinds of space. Space here is synonymous with rooms. We could potentially interchange the words and not lose meaning. So let's look at examples of houses that depart from the tradition of cellular rooms.

Let's take two different houses, one almost but not quite traditional in its composition of rooms and one more flowing and open-plan. Both houses are examples of modernist architecture built in Europe in the early part of the twentieth century, when domestic architecture was being reinvented and when the conventions of eighteenth- and nineteenth-century houses were being upended in the search for new spatial experiences.

I have already introduced the figure of Adolf Loos, an Austrian architect active in the early years of the twentieth century. Loos's houses are particularly useful here because – as well as being rich examples of architecture in their own right – they exist at a threshold between tradition and modernity. Loos is generally regarded as a precursor to modernism, a pioneer and someone who began a reinvention of architecture that was continued in a more radical form by others. His work can therefore be seen as a bridge, somewhere between the traditional arrangement of rooms found in the Victorian house cast by Rachel Whiteread and the more flowing, open-plan arrangements of the twentieth century.

Loos designed the Villa Müller (fig. 15) in Prague in 1930 for a wealthy industrial family. It is a large, bourgeois house in an affluent suburb of the city, and it consists – superficially at least – of a series of traditional rooms with individual functions: dining room, reception room, library, etc. These rooms are treated and decorated in different ways, amplifying the sense of a house made up of discrete, individual and segregated spaces.

And yet Loos also subtly and insistently erodes the walls that separate the main rooms and starts to connect the resulting spaces together. The most important rooms are bounded only on three sides. The fourth enclosing wall is either missing or partially eroded so that one room opens onto the next. Each room is both unique and part of another so that they form a sequence of suggestively inter-connected *spaces*. Sometimes rooms are distinguished by a change of level, using a short flight of steps so that this level change replaces the wall as the main way of differentiating two otherwise distinct functions. The result is a blurring of distinctions between rooms and functions and the introduction of a subtle ambiguity of space.

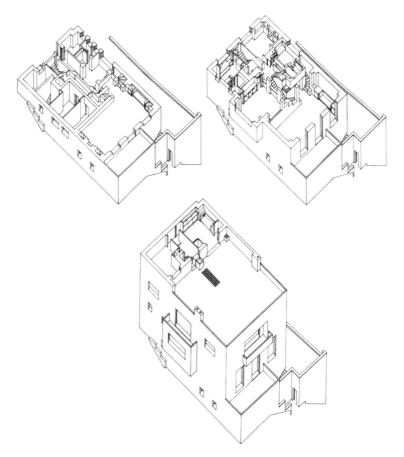

FIG. 15   Diagram and internal view of Villa Müller, Prague, designed by Adolf Loos.

Sometimes Loos shifts both the ceiling and floor levels between rooms. Rather than a series of horizontal floor plates connected by a staircase, his houses are arranged as interlinked volumes. As a result, they tend to have multiple levels and complicated sectional qualities rather than a straightforward ground floor, first floor, etc. Loos did this because he felt that different rooms had different requirements and levels of importance. So his houses became complex, three-dimensional compositions. But he also clearly desired and enjoyed this complexity and the way that, for instance, one room could look partially into another. Changes in ceiling height create moments of compression and release, generating shifts in atmosphere from intimate and contained to grand and expansive.

Loos both reinforced the traditional hierarchy of discrete rooms and undermined it at the same time. His rooms are often decorated in traditional ways, too, using expensive materials such as marble and timber panelling, but the lack of complete separation between each one causes a deliberate disjunction. And the fact that you can see from one room into the next leads to an intriguing sense of heightened awareness, almost a voyeuristic pleasure of looking in. The critic and theorist Beatriz Colomina has compared the interior spaces of Loos's houses to theatre sets. The removal of enclosing walls has the consequence of making his rooms appear like dioramas, spaces in which domestic life is acted out but also spaces that are placed on view. One example serves to illustrate this. The interior of the Villa Müller is dominated by the main reception hall, an elegant, marble-lined space. It is connected to the rest of the house by a complex network of routes and adjoins the dining room, from which it is separated not by a wall but by a screen of marble columns and a short flight of steps. The room is also connected to a tiny reading room located discreetly up another set of side steps via an internal window. The window has the quality of a spyhole, offering a semi-clandestine view from one space to another.

Loos's houses encourage both physical and visual movement, and in doing so they destabilise the 'normal' patterns of discrete rooms. His work helps us to talk about the subtleties of space. There is the space of the room, but also the space between it and the next room. There are private and less private spaces. By partially eroding their traditional separation, Loos turns space into a more tangible entity, something loaded with meaning and suggestive of domestic propriety and social mores. For Loos – as for Whiteread – space has a physical quality: it is something that can be felt. But – unlike Whiteread – it is also something that can be pushed and pulled around, manipulated and massaged. And in this manipulation, space is revealed as something loaded with meaning.

Loos claimed that the real medium of architecture was not the materials and surfaces that defined rooms but the space between them. Loos invented a term – *Raumplan* – for his highly particular way of designing. *Raumplan* is a German compound word that captures his concept of architecture as a three-dimensional composition, a sequence of spaces.

Loos's *Raumplan* is often contrasted with the Swiss architect Le Corbusier's invention of the *plan libre*, meaning free plan. Le Corbusier was born in 1887, a decade and a half after Loos, and his work is generally regarded as a more fully developed version of modern architecture. If Loos's work appears still balanced on the edge of the nineteenth century, Le Corbusier's defines the twentieth century to come. Although their work overlaps, they appear to speak to very different eras and consequently describe very different kinds of space.

Le Corbusier completed the Villa Savoye, a house in the Paris suburbs, in 1931, just a year after the Villa Müller was built. But it presages an entirely different conception of space. The Villa Savoye is generally seen as a more radical building and a more thorough-going exploration of the possibilities of modernism. The ones that concern us here are to do with its spatial design, which is indeed both radical and highly inventive. Le Corbusier explores space as something that flows almost uninhibited through the house.

There are rooms but they are rarely enclosed, and they flow into each other. Circulation is dominant and it unites the house. There is a stair from ground to first floor, but the stronger link is via a ramp that switches back and forth, like a pair of half-open scissors. Space here is seen as something dynamic, and the inhabitation of the house seems to be based on continuous movement. If for Beatriz Colomina the Villa Müller was a theatre, then the Villa Savoye is closer to a cinematic film. Colomina describes the shifts from one space to another within the house as like the jump-cuts in a movie, a series of slices that connect to form a linear, narrative flow.

Much of the Villa Savoye is given over to non-traditional uses. The first floor is only partially enclosed, and the ramp leads to a roof terrace which is open to the sky. Meanwhile, the ground floor of the house is horseshoe-shaped in plan, dominated by a semi-circular curved, glazed wall. The curvature of the glass is based supposedly on the turning circle of cars as they circumnavigate the house before entering the garage, which occupies about half the ground-floor volume. Once again it is movement that determines the spatial layout of the house. Rooms have been almost entirely replaced by something more fluid, something that we might define as pure space. If space is defined by rooms, it is only in the sense that liquid is defined by a glass. Without the containing walls, space can flow, filling up the available volume.

Le Corbusier used ramps in many of his houses. It is a device that erodes vertical separations so that different levels are more closely connected both visually and experientially. If Loos played subtle games with levels and walls, Le Corbusier just blasts right through them. This occurs not only internally but also in the erosion of difference between inside and outside. Le Corbusier's houses sometimes place the garden on the roof and raise the ground floor up so that space flows underneath them. Loos's houses turn a discrete, often rather blank elevation to the street. The invention and the fun and games occur within. Le Corbusier invites the outside in, and by doing so opens up a sense that houses do not just contain space: they exist within it. Space is not just unbounded. Space, it turns out, is everywhere. But that doesn't mean that it is always the same, and it doesn't mean that we all have access to the same amount of it.

We can see in the examples of the Villas Müller and Savoye that spaces can be tangibly different. These buildings show us how space can be understood as something that we can get hold of, manipulate, make flow or dam up, like water. Space is not neutral, though. Turning it into 'stuff' allows us to recognise it as a positive entity, but not perhaps to understand its value or the way that different kinds of space are experienced differently by different people.

Political Space

If you pushed open a green baize door in a passage by my father's study, you entered another passage deceptively similar, but none the less you were on alien ground … one was aware of fear and hate.

In his 1939 essay 'The Lawless Roads', Graham Greene described the experience of growing up in an English public school. Greene's father was the headmaster, and his family lived in a building that contained both their house and the schoolrooms. Separating the two was a green baize door. Greene's anecdote exposes the difference between two kinds of space: domestic and institutional. It also exposes the very different rules that apply in each. Space is not neutral; nor are the differences between spaces merely felt as shifts in mood or feel.

Greene's essay is a travel account of a trip to Mexico in which he describes the effects of the government's anti-Catholic policies. His example of the green baize door is used to highlight the political nature of space and the idea of space as something that can be contested. Loos's interconnected spaces hint at this within the relatively benign arena of domestic life. The interior of the Villa Müller also separates servant areas from those enjoyed by the Müller family. The power relationship between the two can be read in the plan of the house, which relegates servants to the ground floor, away from the main entertaining rooms.

Space is political in the sense that there are political spaces – Trafalgar Square might be termed a political space because it often acts as a focus for political protests – and that it may fall under specific political control. The post-war division of Berlin into American, British, French and Soviet territories is an explicit example of political space. Space here is subject to enforced division, different not in the sense of physical qualities but of ideological difference. Berlin existed before it was divided up. Spatial differences can be seen as arbitrarily imposed rather than designed to be palpably different. But they can also be designed, built into the fabric of buildings and cities.

In London, the Houses of Parliament contain and express the UK's political system. This happens in various ways. In the Commons Chamber itself, where Members of Parliament gather, the arrangement spatially defines the idea of power and opposition. The two parallel and opposing banks of seats enshrine and construct the two-party system. This is demonstrably different from, say, the debating chamber of the European Parliament, which is circular and thus – in theory at least – allows for more than two principal ideological positions.

Space is political in many 'small p' ways, too. Consider the contemporary conversation surrounding the use of public toilets, for instance. Debates between proponents of non-binary definitions of gender and feminists arguing for 'safe spaces' for women make the separation of male and female toilets a highly contentious spatial issue. This is not a question of the shape of a space, or its ambience or its design, but its availability. Space in this sense could be thought of as more like territory, an area that brings into focus questions of ownership, access and rights.

Looked at in this way, all architecture is about territory. Buildings define how much space we have access to and for what reason. We are very used to navigating these issues of access. We know that we can't walk into someone else's house without asking their permission, for instance. And we know that the offices in which we work are divided into all sorts of micro-territories and subsets of a more general space. Power hierarchies within offices, schools and hospitals are legible within the layout and spatial organisation of each. One doesn't need to look at spaces of extreme territory – a disputed war zone or a prison – to understand that space is not universally accessible or the same for everyone.

So space can be regarded as a physical thing, but it is also a cultural and social product, something governed by rules and regulations and divided and subdivided according to questions of ownership and access. This can be very subtle – the difference between the parents' bedroom and the children's bedroom in a house, for instance. Or it can be more insidious. In contemporary housing schemes, the presence of 'poor doors' (entrances for the tenants of affordable or social housing as opposed to those of market rent) is a contemporary manifestation of space as a negotiated and contentious territory.

How does this affect our enjoyment and experience of architecture? How aware are we of these factors? Are they architectural at all, or more a question of social issues that are related to but also somehow 'beyond' architecture? Should we be concerned with them in a book of this nature? Space can be thought of in various ways: as a sensation governed by physical properties, but also as a territory that we navigate according to social rules and conventions. It has different qualities both phenomenological and learned. It is affected by factors that are in themselves not spatial – such as the development of new construction systems – as well as ones that are, such as new forms of family life or patterns of work. Architecture can make sense of these emerging spatial scenarios as much as it draws on those that already exist.

Collage Space

Having introduced the idea of space as something contested and containing political, cultural and social meaning, I would like to return to the question of how we design it. We have already looked at this at the scale of the individual house. Following Alberti, we will now look at the city and the spatial design of urban settlements. It is important to reiterate here that this is a book about experience and about how enjoy architecture, so the examples used are not comprehensive or encyclopaedic. Instead, a few examples have been chosen to elucidate ways in which we experience different urban spaces and how we might approach the experience of others.

Buildings exist in space. What do we mean by this? A city or town or village can be seen as a space itself. The geographic area that settlements exist in can be described in spatial terms. That space might have a specific, overall character as well as subsets or specific territories of space within it. Cities occupy an area of space but not in a uniform way. Any city – no matter where in the world – will be made up of different kinds of space: a cultural area, a business district, residential areas and industrial zones. The nature of these areas will change from city to city, but we can say that human settlements are made of different kinds of spaces.

Different cities have different spatialities. We might call these spaces quarters and we might describe their qualities in different ways, but they are also the product of different ideas about how to design and build cities. Much of the centre of London, for instance, is still based on the small, intimate scale of the medieval city. Attempts to modernise central London, such as Christopher Wren's replanning of the city following the Great Fire, have largely failed. The centre of Paris, on the other hand, is a product of its nineteenth-century reconstruction commissioned by Napoleon III. These spatialities are the product of an accumulation of forces through history, intersections of geography, politics, topography, land ownership, taxes and war. They happen both through design and by accident and through combinations and accumulations of both.

It is beyond the scope of this book to look in detail at the growth of cities and the myriad ways in which they have evolved and the reasons why. But I would like to look at some specific kinds of spatial organisation, and how we might recognise and make sense of the differences. In their influential 1978 book *Collage City*, the historians Colin Rowe and Fred Koetter described what they saw as the difference between the pre-modern and the modern city. They introduced this difference with two contrasting images: one of the internal courtyard of the Uffizi Gallery in Florence, and the other of the Unité d'Habitation, an apartment block in Marseilles designed by Le Corbusier in the 1950s (fig. 16).

Rowe and Koetter chose these two examples because, despite being roughly the same volume, they represent opposing concepts of the city. While Le Corbusier's housing block can be seen as an object floating within the space of the city, the courtyard of the Uffizi is a space defined by buildings around it. If we refer to the earlier example of Rachel Whiteread's *House*, we can see the Unité as the inverse of the Uffizi courtyard, almost as a cast of the space left between the galleries.

Rowe and Koetter's wider point is that modernist urban planning is very different from historical urban planning. If the classical city consisted instead of a series of outdoor rooms, modernism conceived of the city as a space in which objects were placed, almost like sculptures in a gallery or animals in a field. Modernist space is a field, a continuous landscape in which buildings float, a sort of soup into which could be dropped different ingredients.

The pre-modern city represents space as something bounded, more like the rooms of a house, with streets and squares defined as the part left over between the buildings. We started this chapter talking about space as a void between things. If only we could capture it, render it somehow physical, we could understand it. But space can also be seen as something in which we place objects, a field or a territory inhabited by architecture.

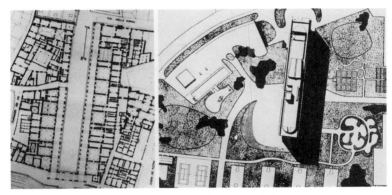

Florence, Uffizi, plan

Le Corbusier: Marseilles, Unité
d'Habitation, 1946, site plan

Unité d'Habitation, view

FIG. 16 Plans and photographs of Unité d'Habitation, designed by Le Corbusier, and the Uffizi Gallery, designed by Giorgio Vasari.

We can feel these differences when we visit different cities. Taking Koetter and Rowe's example, we can imagine a hot afternoon in Florence, moving from the shadows between buildings to the larger spaces of the city's piazzas. Space here does indeed feel like a series of outdoor and indoor rooms, enclosed and bounded by architecture. It is dense, compact, walkable, the very epitome of the civilised notion of the classical city.

We might by contrast imagine the expansive space of a North American city – the wide-open urbanism of Los Angeles, for example, with suburbs spread out at the scale of the vast landscape. It is not simply a question of scale, of pedestrian rather than car traffic, but of space conceived in a totally different way. The differences are not purely ideological or political – although these can be traced – but conceptual too. Space does not exist as an ether into which buildings are dropped but is something we manipulate through our actions. In fact, space is both: it exists without us, but we can shape it, too.

Picturesque Space

If we conceive of space as something all around us, what is its character? What is its shape? Does it vary? How can we change its quality? To answer this, we will briefly leave the city and look instead at the role of spatial design in the landscape. We know that cities are designed and that therefore we can manipulate their form and the way that urban spaces are arranged and experienced. But can the same be said of landscape?

To examine this, we can look at forms of landscape where the hand of designers is most evident. The picturesque gardens of eighteenth-century England offer a specific instance of the evolution in how we think about space in relation to nature. In the seventeenth century, the French landscape garden held sway as the fashionable choice for wealthy Europeans. This style, derived from the formal gardens of the Italian Renaissance, imposed a high degree of order on nature. Gardens became as elaborate and controlled as architecture: external 'rooms' were formed by hedges and planting. Symmetry and geometry are highly evident in the planning of these gardens, which manifest a sense of hierarchy and order.

During the eighteenth century, the fashion shifted towards more natural-seeming schemes. Formal gardens were replaced – literally overlaid – by a different form of spatial organisation. The formal rooms and parterres of the French garden morphed into softly undulating landscapes of apparent naturalness, laid out as seemingly natural parks in which sat large country houses. Various conceptions of beauty fed into a desire for gardens to avoid symmetry and geometry and to mimic the natural landscape instead. Rivers, lakes, clumps of trees and occasional objects of architectural interest including follies and grottoes populated gardens that were in effect no more natural than the formal and ornamental gardens they replaced.

Space was conceived as something that could be manipulated and composed in much the same way as a painting. In fact, these landscapes drew directly on landscape paintings and made the imaginary, two-dimensional worlds depicted by classical painters such as Claude Lorrain and Nicolas Poussin unfold into three-dimensional reality. The picturesque landscape is actually a highly complex space, one designed as a form of entertainment, a spatial *experience* that owners and their guests would use to pass the time. Take the gardens at Studley Royal near Ripon in Yorkshire. Here the landscape is pushed and pulled to create ravines and canyons, wide valleys filled with lakes and twisting, tree-lined routes. Views are formed with earth and enhanced by planting, and into the views are placed objects of fascination. Some of these objects are drawn from classical architecture and from sources around the world, so that the landscapes become allegories of other spaces and places.

The soft folds of these landscapes attempt to appear natural, but they can also be seen as representing an aggressive reshaping of nature. Space here is something manipulable and shaped by aesthetic concerns. The world is literally remade to fit an idea or an image of how it should look. One detail of the picturesque garden serves to highlight this attitude to space. The ha-ha is a device for forming boundaries and edges that are invisible. It is effectively a ditch deployed at the edges of picturesque gardens to stop livestock coming too close to the house while allowing an uninterrupted view of the landscape. The ha-ha allows an idea of the landscape as natural when in fact various very specific controls are being placed on it. It is designed to look undesigned.

What does this tell us about space? Are we not really talking about gardening, the manipulation of landscape and the planting of trees and shrubs? Is this spatial? Underlying the design of gardens by famous landscape designers such as Lancelot 'Capability' Brown and William Kent is an organisation of space around views and routes and territory that can only be described as spatial. Populated for the most part by trees and natural features, such landscapes represent the imposition of a very precise spatial order. It is a spatial order in which we are placed as surely as architecture places us within the rooms of a house.

Equal Space

What is the opposite of the supposed naturalism of the picturesque landscape? Is it something that organises nature into a regular, almost abstract order? Something which demonstrates that space can be divided up rationally and evenly, like a traybake or a page of stamps? The grid is a way of designing that avoids traditional hierarchies. In theory every square on a grid is equal and therefore no one part is more important than any other. The grid is theoretically endless. It is uniform, the same all over. It has no variation and is profoundly unnatural. It has no centre exactly, though it can have edges.

We might associate the grid with cities such as New York or Barcelona, though it only represents a small part of each; in New York it applies to Manhattan alone and in Barcelona it relates only to the nineteenth-century part of the city. But it is the dominant spatial quality of the parts of those cities where it exists. It has an odd effect on navigation, making the city seem both larger and more easily traversed than other, messier or more compromised forms of organisation. It is hard to judge distances in Manhattan. Because we can sometimes see where we are heading, we can ignore just how far away it is. The grid provides a knowability and an ease of comprehension that is also sometimes overwhelming. Maybe we are not used to seeing so much.

Alfred Hitchcock's iconic 'man on the run' film *North by Northwest* begins in Manhattan with a case of mistaken identity. The film's opening credits – designed by Saul Bass – play with grids in a way that mimics the city's spatial organisation. In the film itself, Hitchcock plays with various psychological effects caused by grids, particularly feelings of anonymity and disorientation. His hero, George Kaplan (played by Cary Grant) is mistaken for someone else, as if the character is a square on the grid indistinguishable from any other. The grid also means that Kaplan can slip away, lose himself in Manhattan and escape his pursuers.

Later, the same character ends up in the vast grid of fields in America's Midwestern prairie. Here the endless repetition and wide-open views result in more disorientation, an eerie limitlessness. Neither the size of the gridded fields nor the gridded blocks of Manhattan relate very obviously to the size of a person. Some other scaling up has occurred that is about efficient farming or equally efficient office floor plates. Some of the grid's sense of alienation lies, then, in its abstract lack of human scale, a quality that is usually associated with modernity and twentieth- or late nineteenth-century cities.

But the grid has a long provenance in urban planning. Few places feel as far from New York as New Winchelsea in East Sussex, a small town where the Weald rolls down to the English Channel. This is an ancient-feeling landscape overlooking a bleak stretch of shingle beach. The name New Winchelsea is something of a misnomer. This small town was originally planned out in 1281 on an area of high ground close to the coast. It replaced the previous town of Winchelsea, which was closer to the sea and largely lost to coastal erosion, hence the epithet 'new'.

The town was planned as a grid laid out on top of a hill over-looking the coastal plain below. It is an odd thing: New Winchelsea's grid combined with largely fifteenth- to nineteenth-century houses. The quaintness of East Sussex vernacular materials and ad hoc massing is juxtaposed with an almost abstract sense of space. The grid is palpable, a presence that can be felt. It has an unexpected regularity and a subtle but persistent sense of order. We are used to the jumble of English villages, which have a certain accidental quality. New Winchelsea replaces this with a clarity of spatial design that is unsettling.

Grids might be regular and ordered but they need not always be straight. The city of Milton Keynes (fig. 17) in Buckinghamshire is based on a grid, with each space roughly one kilometre square. This creates a series of districts, each planned slightly differently from the others, connected by a network of roads. But the grid is not uniform and the squares warp to reflect local topography. Here the grid is more like a loose net thrown over a wobbly surface. It is present but less emphatic. The size of the grid makes it unknowable in obvious perceptual terms, though it unmistakably creates a different spatial experience from most cities. Instead of the journey from low-density periphery to high-density centre, Milton Keynes offers for the most part a consistent sense of space, an equality of experience.

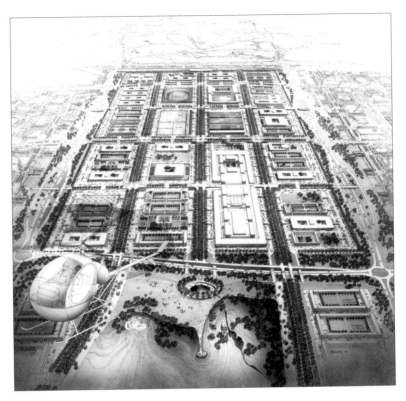

FIG. 17 Aerial view of Milton Keynes, by Helmut Jacoby.

This equality has given rise to a lot of jokes. In the UK, Milton Keynes is sometimes synonymous with a certain kind of boring monotony, an egalitarian but essentially dull uniformity. I happen to like Milton Keynes. It is far odder and more mysterious than its detractors claim. It is a strange fusion of the quirky, pastoral bucolic with a very mid-twentieth-century faith in central planning and bureaucratic organisation. It combines a fascination with North American cities and a devotion to the car with an unexpected English mysticism. The former is represented in the formidable number of roundabouts, while the latter manifests itself in the names of streets such as Midsummer Boulevard.

What is most interesting here, though, is the idea that space can be seen as something that can be manipulated to be fairly and evenly distributed. Milton Keynes's spatial equality is linked to an ideological one. The grid implies that all spaces are equal. We may be on the edge of the grid or somewhere near its centre but there isn't a sense that one is more important than the other. Because architecture is the expression of power in the sense that only people or organisations with some level of power can commission it, its spatiality is part of that power. The spatial organisation of buildings and cities is a product of the social organisation of people.

Utopian Space

From the entire absence of all wynds, courts, and blind alleys, or culs-de-sac, there would be no secret and obscure haunts for the retirement of the filthy and the immoral from the public eye.

JAMES SILK BUCKINGHAM

Milton Keynes was the last of the post-war New Towns in the UK. It marked the end point of an urban and a political experiment. It typified the faith in social democracy of the UK's immediate post-war years. But it is not alone among towns and cities in being planned to represent conceptions of the ideal life. The New Towns of the post-war years grew out of the garden cities of the early twentieth century. Garden cities – effectively the invention of Ebenezer Howard – were an attempt to solve social problems through spatial organisation.

Howard's vision – set out in his book *Tomorrow: A Peaceful Path to Real Reform*, published in 1898 – was based on a fair and egalitarian spatial model, one that allowed for rents to be collected centrally and used for the common good. Howard produced a series of well-known diagrams to explain the rules of spatial governance of his garden city concept, the most famous of which was called 'A Group of Slumless Cities'. It depicts a large circle of space which contains several smaller circular settlements linked by radial roads connected to a single, central city.

The diagram describes a spatial system, but not one that was meant to be literally circular. The circular pattern associated with garden cities is something of a misnomer – no garden city was ever circular – but it provides a powerful spatial metaphor. Howard's idea was really the latest in a long line of spatial ideas for how cities could be planned to improve people's lives.

Take Victoria, a model city designed by James Silk Buckingham in 1849. Victoria was more of an idea than a realistic proposal and it remains unbuilt. Like Howard, Buckingham was not an architect or a planner. He was a journalist, a publisher and a politician. But he wanted to answer society's ills through spatial planning. The organisation of Victoria is a square, measuring one mile by one mile. It is subdivided by eight radial roads, each named after an improving aspiration – Faith, Hope and Charity just to start with. Houses, shops and offices are organised in diminishing squares as the plan marches towards the centre.

In a self-published pamphlet called *National Evils and Practical Remedies*, Buckingham enlarged on the architecture of Victoria, describing in detail the design of balconies and colonnades and the precise use of Corinthian, Ionic and Doric orders of column. Here, the architecture is intended to orchestrate events, establish clear codes of behaviour, delineate class hierarchies and enshrine high-minded social ideals. Buckingham's title makes this purpose clear. Society has created the problems; architecture can solve them.

Victoria is a (relatively) benign version of other spatial experiments during the eighteenth and nineteenth centuries, including prisons, factories and schools. These are buildings that instrumentalise space in the service of an overarching goal to do with control and social organisation. Space here is linked to social betterment and to a sense of order over a chaotic and sometimes anarchic world. Space is a form of control as much as it is place or a territory.

We started this chapter looking at space as a kind of substance, the physical matter formed by Rachel Whiteread's casts of domestic environments. This helped us to understand space as a presence when it is normally perceived as an absence. But it is also misleading. It posits space as something physical that we wade through, a dense liquid we inhabit without agency. But space is also the relationship between objects and people. It is a dynamic, fluid thing, constantly changing and shifting and mutating. The interiors of Adolf Loos and Le Corbusier anticipate social interaction and help construct human relationships. These relationships can be overwritten and subject to change, but they also help to shape us. The houses we inhabit – whether ordinary and generic or special and particular – help to frame our lives. But they also help to construct those lives. We move through space, but it also leaves its imprint on us as we go. Space – however scripted and designed and however much we try to describe and understand it – ultimately remains ambiguous and ineffable.

CHAPTER 4

Materials

T HERE are many ways to begin a chapter on materials in
architecture. We could start with the way that traditional
buildings used the materials that were readily available. We might
list the typical materials that buildings have been made of in different
regions and cultures. We could approach the question of materials
from a technical point of view, describing their role in terms of how
they perform structurally or thermally.

The question of materials in architecture is complex. It represents an intersection of issues, of the practical and the symbolic,
the structural and the ornamental, the pragmatic and the creative.
Materials are chosen not just for their physical capabilities, economic
viability, easy availability or aesthetic values. Sometimes all these
factors come into play, to varying degrees. Sometimes materials
are chosen not because they lie easily to hand but because they are
rare or valuable.

The availability of materials has shaped the way building styles
have evolved, but not always in a straightforward or linear manner.
Every building uses materials from a variety of sources, some
closer to home than others. But different buildings merit different
approaches. The use of more exotic materials has often represented
a display of wealth or importance, for example. Materials are chosen
to express certain aspects that are important for the building, and
in doing so they are sometimes used in unexpected ways. Buildings
that appear to be made of one thing are sometimes made of quite

another. And buildings that look flimsy or cheaply constructed might be in some ways closer to expressing an honesty of construction than those that strive to look solid and timeless.

Geography and geology will form part of this discussion, but we will also look at style and taste as well as fashion and trends in building. The suitability of a material has to do with ideas of visual decorum as well as physics, with the aspirations of a building's owner and those of the community in which it is a part. What buildings are made of has a lot to do with how we want buildings to look and feel and what we ultimately want them to say about us. A discussion about materials in architecture therefore comes with a lot of baggage. It is never simply a question of performance. Materials carry symbolic as well as physical weight. They hold up ideas as much as buildings.

This chapter takes a simple format: it is divided into sections looking at specific materials. Each one allows us to think about wider questions of material choice. Like the other chapters in the book, therefore, it will move around a bit, choosing examples from different periods and places to explore the intersection of structural logic, symbolic value, physical availability, legislation, economics and other factors that influence the choice of materials in architecture. We will begin with a seemingly everyday material – clay or ceramic tiles – and through them introduce the issue of authenticity, a word that hovers in the background of almost all material questions.

Tiles (Mathematical and Otherwise)

One of the supposed central tenets of modernist architecture was that materials should be true to themselves and that buildings should be made of what they appear to be. It would be truer perhaps to say that this tenet became an assumption around modern architecture without ever being precisely true. But structural and material honesty remains a persuasive and pervasive argument. It feels – on the face of it – self-evident. How can materials *not* be what they appear to be? And why would anyone – a designer, a client, an owner – want to use fake materials or suggest a building was made of something that it wasn't?

But buildings are quite often made of materials that aren't all they appear to be. Let's take a relatively obvious example. Mathematical tiles were a popular building material in southern England in the eighteenth and nineteenth centuries. If you take a walk around the town of Lewes in East Sussex (fig. 18), for example, you will see a lot of mathematical tiles, quite possibly without being aware of them.

FIG. 18 A house in Lewes.

Mathematical tiles are – essentially – fake bricks. They are made of clay and fired in the same way that normal bricks are, but they are hung on the side of a building rather than used structurally. They are stuck onto the façade to make it look like it is made of brick when it isn't. The tiles don't hold anything up other than themselves, but when mortared in place they look remarkably convincing. The tell-tale signs are subtle, but once you are aware of them, they become quite easy to spot. Because the tiles are not holding anything up, they don't have lintels or arches over window or door openings, and because they are very thin, their exposed edges are often covered up by strips of timber at the corners. So rather than turning around a corner – as normal, load-bearing bricks do – mathematical tiles often clad the front façade of a building only, giving way to other materials on less important elevations.

Why would someone use mathematical tiles rather than real bricks? The answer is a combination of changing methods of construction and cycles of fashion and taste. I have already said that geographic availability is one of the factors governing the choice of building materials. Historically, buildings tended to be made of the materials that were easily to hand. Building materials therefore shifted from region to region depending on the underlying geology and land uses. In areas like Sussex that had relatively little in the way of stone but lots of trees, houses were mostly made from timber. Many of the older houses in Lewes are timber-framed and date from the fifteenth to the seventeenth century. The space between the timbers would invariably have been filled with plaster, or sometimes bricks, so that the frame would remain expressed and the structure of the building legible.

During the eighteenth century this look became unpopular and timber-framed houses were refurbished to look more typical for the Georgian period, which favoured brick and stone. These materials often came from further afield and were therefore representative of an industrialising construction process. Georgian builders brought stone and bricks from elsewhere, updating existing houses. Sometimes the bricks were substituted by mathematical tiles, which gave the illusion of a brick façade to a building that was held up by timber framing.

Mathematical tiles have a contemporary counterpart in the façade panels that clad many modern buildings. But the use of tiles in architecture has a long history. Perhaps because they are always applied and never structural, tiles can be regarded as somehow less noble or honest than other materials. They cover surfaces rather than articulate what things are made of. The beautiful blue tiles that adorn the elevations of many buildings in Portugal – a product of the influence of Muslim and Arabic architecture – offer a spectacular case in point. The depiction of religious scenes where whole façades become pictures ignores the reality of the architecture behind. Windows, doors and other features merely interrupt these images, like holes intruding into a canvas. The abstract patterned tiles also have their own scale and logic, which – like wallpaper – is indifferent to the materials they cover.

When I worked on the design of A House for Essex – a building on the Essex coast completed in 2014 – with the artist Grayson Perry, we decided to cover the entire exterior of the building in tiles. Cast in terracotta and glazed in green and white, the tiles depicted specific, symbolic content relating to the story of the house as well as forming an all-over pattern across its surface. This was a project that gloried in pattern, decoration and storytelling in architecture. Like the façade of a Portuguese church, the tiles told a story and formed a richly decorative language. Unlike Portuguese tiles, they were large and heavy, so they weren't glued but bolted in place. They relate to a history of faience tiles, which not only clad the vertical surfaces of a building but also form an intricate and complex three-dimensional surface of their own.

Stone

Castle Drogo is often referred to as the last castle built in Britain. It was commissioned by Julius Drewe, a wealthy entrepreneur, and completed in 1930. Drewe wanted a baronial, ancestral home and so he did what any self-made millionaire would do and built one from scratch. His castle was designed by Sir Edwin Lutyens and built on a dramatic site on Dartmoor in Devon. Lutyens's original design was for a stone-faced building that also had a cavity to allow the stone to drain. But Drewe insisted that his castle should be built as medieval castles had been: that is, out of solid, load-bearing stone. The result is that the walls of Castle Drogo are permanently wet. The rain lashing in across the moors is driven against and through the stone. Without a cavity – and without any insulation in that cavity – the walls are wet on the inside and the outside and Castle Drogo is both cold and damp. An authentic castle, you might say, and Drewe got what he wanted (and perhaps deserved).

So Castle Drogo looks authentic, but isn't, because it is not really a castle. Lutyens translated the castellations, bastions, towers and arrow slits into an abstract language, something that looked *castle-like* without really being one. Its solid granite stone, load-bearing and unyielding, is both real and an illusion – which begs a question or exposes a prejudice about materials, one that equates solid and heavy materials with truth. This preference can partially be explained by a desire for buildings to be safe and secure. Heavy materials will surely provide better shelter than light ones. But as Castle Drogo shows, this is not necessarily true, particularly because buildings need to do more than merely stand up and materials must do more than resist erosion or carry load. It can be a bad idea for the inside of a building to be made of the same as the outside. Julius Drewe, sitting damp and freezing in his twentieth-century castle, discovered that to his cost.

Even when buildings are made of traditional materials, these might be used in non-traditional ways. One of the reasons that contemporary buildings are often not made of what they might appear to be made of – their external material expression – has to do with increasingly sophisticated ways to make buildings watertight and thermally efficient. Contemporary buildings are made of many layers, of different materials doing different things. Let's look at a much more recent building than Castle Drogo but one that nonetheless shares some of its characteristics. No. 1 Poultry (fig. 19) is a mixed-use building in the City of London. It was designed in the 1980s (though not completed until 1997) by the architecture practice of James Stirling, Michael Wilford and Partners.

FIG. 19 No. 1 Poultry, London, designed by James Stirling.

No. 1 Poultry is a steel-framed building, clad externally in two different types of stone laid in alternating bands to form a pattern of stripes. The stone, though, is not load-bearing and is effectively clipped to the frame behind it. As this method of fixing doesn't need mortar to bond different courses of stone together, the gaps behind the blocks have been left open. These gaps have the effect of making the stone appear to be floating, defying our expectation that a heavy material needs to support itself by being stacked, one block on top of another.

There is a term for this way of cladding buildings. A rain-screen cladding doesn't quite do what its name suggests. It forms the external surface of a building and thus protects it from the worst of the weather. But rain is also allowed to pass through and behind, where it will meet a waterproof sheeting, hidden behind the cladding, which is what keeps the rest of the building dry. Rainwater runs down the surface of this sheet, behind the cladding, and drains away. A ventilation gap allows the space to dry out so that the cladding is set some way in front of the structure of the building, which lurks behind. This structure might be load-bearing masonry – bricks or concrete blocks – or it might be a frame made of concrete, steel or timber. But it is not the same as the material that forms the building's surface. This gives rise to a sense that things are not what they seem.

No. 1 Poultry is an eloquent and clever example of this means of constructing a building, one that articulates the contradictions of its apparent materiality. It appears to want things both ways: to seem both massive and solid as well as light and layered. We know that the stone used on many contemporary buildings is not what is holding the building up, but it is usually presented to us as if it is. No. 1 Poultry celebrates the conceit, enjoys the 'lie' and reveals the truth. It also uses its principal facing material – stone – to achieve something else, which is polychromatic decoration. Here the contrasting bands of stone produce an overall decorative effect that has nothing to do with constructional need but a lot to do with the ornamental potential of stone.

We have already discussed Alberti's contribution to Renaissance architecture in the form of his Palazzo Rucellai. In 1450, the same family commissioned Alberti to decorate the façade of the medieval basilica of Santa Maria Novella. Alberti developed the language of classical architecture into a rich polychromatic surface of green and white marbles. Alberti's forms both relate to the existing Gothic chapel and develop an entirely new classical language of architecture. What he created is an extravagantly beautiful surface, an exquisite drawing in stone depicting niches, scrolls, columns and pilasters – a surface that is both part of and completely detached from the building behind it.

It would be unfair to leave stone at this point, branded as a material associated with artifice and illusion, however beautifully wrought. So we will look briefly at a building where its solidity and structural integrity is most tangibly expressed.

The Danish architect Jørn Utzon is most famous for designing the Sydney Opera House. But that extraordinary and iconic building is unrepresentative of much of his other work, which was altogether introspective in character. The house he built for his family in 1971 on the rocky south coast of Mallorca in Spain is a far more telling and eloquent example. Can Lis is a house that is both austere and lavish. The lavishness comes from the intensity and lack of compromise with which Utzon handled the house's principal material: marés stone. This golden sandstone forms all the principal walls of the house along with its floor, columns and dressings. There are no stud walls or lightweight screens, very few painted surfaces and no obvious decoration. The stone is used in large chunks, raw and unpolished. Other materials are involved – the openings are formed from expressed steel beams, and benches and tables are clad in sharply coloured and patterned ceramics which pop like op art patterns against the earthy background. But the stone provides the principle of the house, which wants to appear as a kind of refined and sculpted version of the rocks on which it sits. It is an extreme and uncompromising experience, ostentatious and primal. There are no cavities in Utzon's walls, no hint of sham. However, this lack of compromise was not without its problems: the steel supports and the unadorned stone suffer erosion in the salty and abrasive coastal climate. Like Castle Drogo, the marés stone lets in water. The romance of solid stone can come at a cost.

Stucco and Plaster

Georgian houses were made from many things, not all of them particularly wholesome. They tended to reserve the best bricks for the front of a house and used 'bungaroosh' – a crude, concrete-like building material that incorporated all sorts of broken bricks, lumps of stone and other loose odds and ends – for the back and sides. Another solution was to cover all the elevations with a layer of plaster or 'stucco'. That way it didn't really matter what buildings were actually made of.

The outer circle of London's Regent's Park is lined by the creamy stucco façades of John Nash's terraces. They provide an elegant but skin-deep backdrop to the leafy abundance of the park itself. Likewise, the Regency façades of Brighton reveal the eighteenth-century growth of this seaside city. The creamy stucco that covers their gently curving surfaces catches the light and forms great billowing elevations.

Nash's Regent's Park buildings appear to be large houses facing onto their own grounds, composed around implied central pedimented entrances. In fact, the apartments are accessed from the back and the composition of the façades responds to an illusory sense of grandeur. The stucco is sometimes scored in order to suggest stone, but really it gives the buildings an a-scalar quality: the blocks are irreducible to the individual components from which they are made. Windows and doors can be manipulated to some extent, but individual bricks can't.

Nash's work is scenographic, concerned with overall visual effects rather than detail. The underlying materials of building aren't important. On the fact of it this would seem as far as one can get from the honesty of material expression that we discussed at the start of this chapter. But that depends on which early modernism one looks at. If we took the purist villas of Le Corbusier, the series of houses that he designed in the 1920s and early 1930s, we could see some similar things happening at the level of material. Le Corbusier's early houses

FIG. 20 Plasterwork in Kenwood House, London, designed by Robert Adam.

have a machine-like quality, a beautiful purity and sharpness. Their exteriors are predominantly made up of white planes punctured by strip windows and held up by circular piloti columns.

The whiteness is only skin deep, though. The walls of Le Corbusier's villas are made from masonry, blockwork and brickwork, which is then rendered to give it an illusion of smooth, abstract planes. His buildings look modern, but they rely on traditional construction methods. There is nothing wrong with rendered surfaces, or with covering up one material with another. But both Le Corbusier's villas and Nash's terraces rely on the thinness of materials to achieve their most singular characteristics. Here, material is not about structure but about surface. Material in architecture is not only what holds a building up but also what we want it to look like.

Stucco, plaster and render are not confined to the exterior of buildings. We have already looked at the work of Robert Adam in terms of the spatial configuration of his houses. But his interiors include incredibly refined decorative plaster surfaces, too. Adam took the decorative language of classical architecture, the mouldings and profiles of stone construction, and developed it into elegant and delicate plaster patterns that define walls and ceilings. Placed against pastel-painted walls, his patterns of medallions, ceiling roses, borders, frames and foliage have the quality of the finest pottery, sublime decorative confections that cover every surface (fig. 20).

Brick

Both Nash's terraces and Le Corbusier's purist villas cover up the material their buildings are made of in favour of an overall effect. The desire for a seamless surface trumps the materials used to form that surface. There is, though, another school of thought, one that tries to express material honesty and reveal the method of construction.

In an infamous lecture to his students at Yale University, the influential post-war American architect Louis Kahn once famously held up a brick and asked it what it wanted to be. It is not recorded if the brick provided an answer, but the question suggested that all materials have a true role, an authentic way to be used that suits their innate properties. In his buildings, Kahn left his bricks exposed for all to see. Kahn strived to express materials in as raw a state as possible, in such a way that the method of their construction became the expressive quality of the architecture.

This might suggest that his buildings are overly literal and pragmatic, or somewhat one-dimensional. But instead they are rich and multivalent, layered and complex. They possess an unmistakable sculptural power. With Kahn, the weight of rhetoric and of reverence can be off-putting. His words have a mystical quality, even a pomposity, but his buildings are undeniably present and impressive.

Much of this presence comes down to his emphatic use of materials, particularly brick. Kahn's design for the Indian Institute of Management in Ahmedabad is an extraordinarily powerful building, almost primitive in a way that contemporary buildings generally aren't. It is difficult to imagine this building having anything as prosaic as a function – indeed, that might be part of its problem and why it was recently only narrowly saved from demolition. It feels more like something once used but now in partial ruination. It has a primal quality and an emptiness, as if all the unnecessary, everyday things that buildings must do have been abandoned, leaving only a raw, exposed shell.

The bricks here are piled up relentlessly to form vast slabs of wall, unrelieved by other niceties. Openings are formed by brick arches or by raw concrete lintels that sit on the bricks at the corners in a striking example of elemental construction methods. Openings seem to have no glass, which serves only to emphasise the depth of the brick and the primal qualities of the building. Kahn developed a theory about layering, wrapping buildings in walls so that the outer layer acts simply as a screen, a vestigial relic of architecture that has little to do other than be. Freed from the obligations of enclosing practical space, these walls become rhetorical, suggestive of a degree-zero form of architecture.

The Yale University Art Gallery in downtown New Haven is an earlier building by Kahn and an exercise in matter-of-fact bluntness in materials, even if it displays a subtlety of planning and spatial composition. Kahn's work – at least in this building – can be seen as a way of returning architecture to an idea of essence. Each element is employed to articulate and express its essential qualities. Bricks are piled up to make walls. Concrete lintels span openings. Deep beams span across spaces.

Kahn's architecture is both rich and austere. His buildings are contemporary and archaic, carrying the aloof ambiguity of inhabited ruins. Kahn used concrete in similarly elemental ways, but the brick of the Ahmedabad buildings has a textural warmth and an earthiness alongside the sculptural power. When Kahn asked the brick what it wanted to be, the answer turned out not to be a building as such but the remains of a previous architecture.

It is hard to make modern buildings look as simple as Kahn's do. In fact, it takes a lot of work and, quite often, a high degree of artifice. Kahn's work was especially influential on the architectural movement known as Brutalism. This is mostly associated with the use of reinforced concrete but, strictly speaking, Brutalism is an approach founded on a desire for the honest and straightforward use of materials. This honesty is linked to ideas around simplicity and a beauty that comes from humble things. Bricks are no more honest than marble blocks or polished mahogany, so what is being communicated here is an *idea* of honesty.

The work of the husband-and-wife team of Alison and Peter Smithson is instructive in any description of Brutalism. They were the authors of an influential essay in 1956 entitled 'But Today We Collect Ads' in which they set out a response to the emerging consumer culture of the post-war era. What the Smithsons pre-scribed was something they termed a 'rough poetry', a tough, no-nonsense and unsentimental architecture that was also honest. Their Sugden House, built in 1955 in Watford on the edge of London, epitomised this approach.

To all intents and purposes, the Sugden House looks like an ordinary, detached suburban residence. Not particularly large, made of stock brick with a pitched roof, it appears at first almost boringly normal. But the house packs a punch that is made more powerful by being so subtle. The standard, metal-framed windows form odd, disconcertingly unresolved patterns across the façade. They appear to be in the wrong places, leaving worryingly thin strips of brickwork between them. The roof is asymmetrical, coming down low at the back, which is also the entrance. Inside, the ground floor is mostly open-plan, with kitchen units and a chimney breast taking on the role of the walls in giving a sense of order to the spaces. Materials are left raw and exposed. There is bare brick, rough concrete lintels, off-the-peg fittings and cables fixed straight to the surfaces. It is calculatedly raw, abrasively rough and ready. The architecture is – in terms of the spatial games being played – extremely sophisticated, but the materials are deliberately normal. It is like an aesthetic response to the austerity of rationing, a sense of studied frugality. More than the flamboyant concrete structures associated with Brutalism, the Sugden House nails the principles of the movement.

Brick is not always used to achieve uniformity or solidity. It can be highly decorative and richly ornamental. The diaper (or diamond) patterns of Tudor brickwork, where dark grey bricks are contrasted against a background of red brick, were revived during the late Victorian period by architects such as George Devey who were interested in their polychromatic effect. Devey used brick to make buildings of great complexity and historical resonance, often suggestive of structures that had grown over time. His 1878 design for St Albans Court, a country house in east Kent built for the banker William Oxenden Hammond, combined patterned brickwork with stone laid to suggest that a new house had emerged from the ruins of a much older one, a Victorian house evoking an Elizabethan mansion built from the remains of a medieval structure. Bricks used picturesquely and in various bonds – the pattern in which the bricks are laid – became Devey's method for constructing elaborate fictive histories for his new houses.

The façade of numbers 26 and 27 Cowcross Street in London, a pair of warehouses designed in 1827 by Thomas Milburn, is a sublime example of the decorative potential of brick. Different bricks are laid in various bonds and patterns to achieve variety and contrast, delineating arches, floor levels and horizontal banding. Milburn draws on Italian Renaissance and Gothic sources to animate an otherwise regular grid of windows and openings. It is at once an ordinary commercial Victorian building and an extraordinary piece of decorative façade-making.

Steel

The materiality of the Sugden House was a calculated snub to the polite mainstream of modernism at the time. In their earlier design for a secondary school in Hunstanton, Norfolk, the Smithsons combined their emerging Brutalist aesthetic of using materials in as basic way as possible with steel-frame construction. This problematic building, which suffered from overheating and other issues, was also a homage to the work of Mies van der Rohe, the poet of the steel frame. Unlike the rather rough-and-ready Hunstanton School, Mies's work is highly refined and luxurious in its materiality. His most famous building was one that lasted just a handful of weeks, a building that became a phantom within the history of modern architecture, exerting an enormous, mysterious pull based on a handful of black-and-white photographs.

Mies designed the Barcelona Pavilion for the 1929 International Exposition in Barcelona in collaboration with Lilly Reich (fig. 21). It was a remarkable piece of architecture, an elegant, minimal structure clad in the most opulent and exquisite of materials. It was made up of a series of horizontal planes, with a thin, oversailing roof hovering above a beautiful, travertine base. Slender chrome columns offer unlikely support to the roof because they seem barely there themselves. Slabs of pink onyx marble slide across the plan, loosely defining spaces if not exactly rooms. There are glass screens and a shallow pool and more walls of shiny green marble and a play of light, reflections and layers of transparency and opacity that produces an exquisitely refined experience. Here is an architecture of beautiful surfaces and flowing spaces, of luxurious materials and refinement. When there is something as mundane as a curtain, it is a deep red, floor-to-ceiling billowing wall of fabric, the kind of curtain that would swoosh without resistance across the space.

As a building it could not be more different from Hunstanton School, though it used precisely the same technology. Its steel

FIG. 21 Barcelona Pavilion, Barcelona, designed by Mies van der Rohe.

structure was mostly hidden, allowing the architecture to concentrate on remarkable spatial and material effects. When Mies later moved to the USA and designed large office buildings and apartments, he took his love of steel construction with him. His most famous post-war work is the Seagram Building in Manhattan. The Seagram is also made of a steel frame infilled with deep bronze-framed slabs of glass. Fire regulations meant that the steel frame had to be encased, though, so Mies stuck additional but unnecessary steel sections on the exterior to communicate what the building was made of. Here, the honest material of the steel structure becomes a piece of applied symbolism. Truth is sacrificed for effect.

Glass

For something transparent and not quite there, glass is an extremely important material. It is associated with contemporary architecture, but its historical role is also important. Hardwick Hall is a late Elizabethan mansion in Derbyshire in the UK, built to the designs of Robert Smythson though with considerable input from his client, Bess of Hardwick, in the 1590s. New Hardwick Hall, to give it its proper title, was the fourth house commissioned by Bess and by far the most ambitious and elaborate. It is extraordinary, the most striking aspect of it being the vast windows – made from many small squares of glass held in lead frames – that become taller and more stretched as each floor progresses. 'Hardwick Hall, more window than wall' goes the saying, and here the extent of glazing is directly linked to the self-belief of the building's owner. Her initials are placed in carved giant letters on the parapet of the building, asserting its importance. Hardwick is a 'prodigy house', a term developed by the critic Sir John Summerson to describe the kind of sumptuous and impressive houses built to host and entertain Elizabeth I as she travelled the country. Hardwick is the most sumptuous and impressive of them all, and a large part of this is to do with the technical achievement of those huge windows. Of all the materials of modern architecture, it is glass that seems to encapsulate both its optimism and its limitations. Glass is closely tied to technology, representing a journey from internalised protective spaces to expansive and outward-looking ones. Sheets of glass get bigger through the history of architecture, glass manufacturing technology seeming to enable a sense of architecture's own expansiveness. We can trace the development of glass through Tudor, Georgian and Victorian architecture, individual panes becoming larger until we arrive in the twentieth century and the expansive sheets of unbroken glass of modernism.

Mies van der Rohe designed the Villa Tugendhat in Brno, in what was then Czechoslovakia, in 1930. It continued many of the same themes as his Barcelona Pavilion, but this time it offered a space not purely for contemplation but one to be lived in. Despite this pragmatic demand, the Villa Tugendhat is an architecture of unbridled luxury, one offering opulent surfaces and a sense of limitlessness brought on by material reflections and the dissolution of boundaries. The house appears in fictional form in Simon Mawer's 2009 novel *The Glass Room*. Here it is reduced to its dominant material. The glass in the real Villa Tugendhat was electronically controlled: its giant picture window could descend into the floor to reveal an unbroken connection with the landscape beyond. In Mawer's novel, the glass takes on all sorts of metaphorical roles, emblematic of a desire for transparency that masks various forms of deceit, and redolent of an optimism destroyed by events.

Glass means transparency and a desire for openness, of a kind. Mawer's novel places glass as the quintessential material of modern architecture. There is a real glass house too, or at least a real house called the Glass House. This was designed by Philip Johnson, an American post-war acolyte of Mies. Johnson designed the house for himself on his Connecticut estate in 1948. Two horizontal slabs of steel are raised above the ground. Between them extend sheets of glass and ... not much more. A modicum of privacy is granted to the bathroom, which is enclosed within a circular brick drum in the centre of the plan. There is one wall, more of a screen really, which separates the sleeping area from the rest of the space. And that is it. Johnson lived in almost aristocratic splendour on his estate, where his uninterrupted glass walls were unlikely to be troubled by anyone looking in.

The American artist Dan Graham was fascinated by the psychological complexities of glass and its role in modern architecture. Graham made a series of pavilions that use transparent and mirror glass to play complex, perceptual games with viewers. He also designed his own glass house, a conceptual intervention into American post-war housing. In a project titled *Alteration to a Suburban House* (1978), Graham took a typical post-war detached house and removed its front, street-facing wall. He replaced it with a vast single sheet of glass. The interior, rear wall of the house was replaced with a mirror. The interior thus became a public event, reflected to the occupants of the house as well as to any passers-by. Graham took the supposed neutrality of the glass house and the large picture window and exposed its complex voyeuristic tendencies. The family inside his conceptual house is on show.

Glass is not a neutral material, and neither is it entirely transparent. It reflects things, and one of the things it reflects is confidence. One has to be confident to live in a glass house. Mies's Seagram Building turns architecture inside out. By day it seems to disappear, reflecting its surroundings, and by night, it turns its interior into the exterior: the office layouts of its thirty-eight floors become lit stage sets. Something very similar happens in the less glamorous location of Ipswich in Suffolk. The Willis Faber & Dumas office building there, designed by Norman Foster in the mid-1970s, is a sinuous curve of glass that follows the curving street line. By day it reflects its surroundings in a fragmented picture of the neighbouring streets. At night, with the lights on, it becomes transparent. At neither point is it quite there.

Concrete

If there is one material that is most obviously associated with modern architecture, it is concrete. This connection is stylistic but also more general. Concrete is both ubiquitous and unpopular. It is often used as a pejorative term to describe unwanted contemporary development generally: 'concreting over the countryside' and 'concrete jungle' are examples of how concrete is frequently conflated with ugliness.

In the UK, concrete is routinely decried as a particularly unsuitable material, one that stains easily due to the climate, becoming grim and oppressive. Walk through almost any UK town and there will invariably be one obviously concrete building, probably built in the 1950s or 1960s and for public or civic use. So what is the attraction? Is there anything good to say about it beyond its expedient, pragmatic value? It is difficult to imagine most routine building occurring without it. We use it to make foundations and floors, even when the resulting building hides the material away. It is relatively cheap, immensely practical and forgiving to work with – none of which describes its attraction or, equally, why it is so disliked.

Concrete's principal attraction for architects is its physical versatility. Strengthened by steel reinforcement bars, it can perform extraordinary structural feats. Unlike brick or stone, you don't need to stack one bit on top of another. You can make shapes, extend floors as cantilevers, project buildings out of thin air. You can cast it into almost any shape. This gives it an incredible plastic virtuosity. Once you realise this, all those concrete buildings start to make more sense. They don't need to act like traditional buildings made of load-bearing materials, so why should they?

It is hard to think of a more extreme expression of the capabilities of concrete construction than the São Paulo Museum of Art designed in the late 1960s by Lina Bo Bardi (fig. 22). A vast concrete frame, painted blood red, supports a heavily glazed space hanging between the columns. It was the largest free span in the world when it was completed in 1968. The gallery floors act like a bridge suspended by the concrete frame and accessed by a staircase rising from the podium below. It is a breathtaking object that follows very little of architecture's traditional conventions. It has little relationship to the street. It has no obvious elevations in the accepted sense, no composition of windows and walls. It has no decoration and no obvious concession to craft or the resolution of details. Close up, it is rough and even crude, but it is undeniably spectacular and sophisticated as both a gesture and an experience.

Concrete lends itself to both dramatic, sculptural gestures and a vastly different conception of architecture from traditional building. Instead of simple relations between building, street and elevation,

FIG. 22   São Paulo Museum of Art, designed by Lina Bo Bardi.

concrete construction reinterprets the city as a sculptural land-scape, a space of strata and levels, ramps and walkways. Take the Barbican Estate in central London. Conceived originally in the 1950s, designed by Chamberlin, Powell and Bon and constructed over a period of some thirty years, the Barbican is an extraordinary piece of city-making. Here, standard spatial navigation is rejected in favour of a multi-levelled landscape where buildings merge with ramps and walkways. Walking through the Barbican can be a dis-orienting experience. Buildings are both above and below you. Trees grow from podiums with car parks below. Ramps start off inside buildings before bursting out of them and then back in again. The entrance to a building might be several metres up and accessed by a bridge. The street is not really a valid category.

The Barbican is notoriously confusing, and getting lost is par for the course. It is undoubtedly frustrating for first-time visitors, and is often described as alienating and unsuccessful as a piece of city-making. It is also undoubtedly thrilling, full of unexpected spatial encounters, remarkable views, vistas and inventiveness. This is not just enabled by concrete but somehow made conceptually possible by it. The material infuses every corner of the Barbican. Sometimes it is massive and heavy-looking – extensive pick-ham-mering gives much of the estate the look of an elephant's hide – but it is also expressed as thin barrel vaults and projecting balconies. It is curved and sometimes surprisingly sensuous but also sharp and honed into angles and aggressive cantilevers. Very little of it is covered up or prettified. Instead it dominates, expressing its dynamic potential. Concrete's omnivorous appetite is not confined to structural and spatial games but includes a stylistic eclecticism. The Barbican is a riot of architectural references from vernacular Greek hillside towns to Roman amphitheatres to the furious classical imagination of Piranesi.

Concrete may not enjoy widespread popularity, but it enables architecture to escape from the straitjacket of streets and façades and to become something more organic, more ambitious, more like a sculptural landscape than a city of objects. It can change our relationship to space and to site, sending us up, around and over buildings in a physical, haptic experience. Some people dislike it for this reason, for breaking the basic rules of building and simple ideas of orientation. They also dislike it for more pragmatic reasons, for its ubiquity perhaps and for the way that it ages and shows the signs of weathering and time. It can indeed be grey and oppressive and somewhat unrelenting. It has no obvious scale unless the architect gives it one. But it can also be dynamic and thrilling, opening architecture up to vertiginous experiences and a freedom to follow an idea to its extreme.

Plastic

Plastic is not a material one normally associates with buildings, especially not positively. I wouldn't claim that it has a long and illustrious history. Nor is it particularly popular today. But it is important in terms of thinking about the evolution of building materials and how these are sometimes adopted by architects to do interesting things.

Plastic is present in buildings in all sorts of ways. Behind the brickwork of most new houses, for instance, is a plastic-based layer called a breather membrane that keeps the interior dry and allows the building to breathe. Below the floor is another sheet called a damp-proof membrane that also laps up the side of the walls to form a sort of protective tub in which the dry parts of the house sit. Plastic parts tend to have these kinds of dry, technical names because they perform dry, technical tasks. Numerous other parts and accessories such as extractor units, tubes, pipework, insulation, light switches and consumer boxes populate the construction of our houses, alongside the increasingly ubiquitous uPVC windows.

We don't tend to talk about these elements much in architectural conversations, but they are necessary and for the most part they do their job well.

But plastic, rubber and related products have also made less furtive appearances when architects have attempted to use new industrial processes to make buildings. We have already encountered Alison and Peter Smithson in their down-to-earth, Brutalist guise with the Sugden House, but they also designed the vastly different House of the Future, a prototype for modern living exhibited at full scale in the 1956 Ideal Home Show at London's Olympia (fig. 23). The Smithsons' design was a moulded plastic interior, a sort of inhabited amoeba, filled with electronic gizmos including tables that rise from the floor and a remote-control-operated bath. The design explored an idea of architecture as a product utilising contemporary industrial techniques rather than relying on the comparatively antiquated method of piling up bricks or assembling timber frames.

It's an appealing idea: we mass produce most consumer products, why not houses? Mass production would in theory remove

FIG. 23 House of the Future, designed by Alison and Peter Smithson.

the kind of mistakes and errors that occur in one-off construction, bringing efficiencies and aspects of choice and flexibility. For various reasons – often to do with the complexities of individual sites and circumstances – this dream of mass-produced housing has never been fulfilled. Most houses in the UK are built using relatively primitive methods, assembled by people on site using traditional materials. Aspects of mass production are involved in the components that go into building and the methodologies employed by developers to introduce greater efficiencies, but that is usually as far as it goes. Adventures in plastics remain few and far between.

One example can be found on the outskirts of Haslemere in Surrey. Surrounded by trees and attached to a late Victorian country house is the former Olivetti Training Centre, completed in 1972. The extension was designed by James Stirling in typically rumbunctious style. Two angled wings are linked to each other and to the older house by a fragmented, glazed structure. The wings are made of glass-reinforced plastic (GRP) and have alternating bands of cream and beige. The GRP is moulded so there are no sharp edges – the building has the vacuum-formed quality of the office products such as typewriters and calculators made by Olivetti.

Stirling's original designs for the GRP proposed a more acidic colour scheme of alternating purple and green strips. As it was, these colours were confined to the interior. The exterior looks like a high-tech Battenberg cake, as if it could be sliced up easily and served on a plate. It is both cute and confusing, sleek in places but also awkward in the relationship of its parts. The windows are horizontal slits with curved corners, like those of a train carriage, and the ends of each wing are abrupt, as if another few carriages – or slices of Battenberg – could be added.

The building was not without its technical problems, and Stirling's other experiments in GRP – most notably his Southgate Estate housing in Runcorn New Town, which was demolished some fifteen years after it was built – spelt the end of his use of the material. The failings of Runcorn were not down to the GRP – though it did earn the estate the nickname of 'Legoland' because of its bright, plasticky character – but it is a material that is often associated with problems, aesthetic as much as technical.

Both the Smithsons' House of the Future and Stirling's Olivetti building were an attempt to make architecture out of materials that reflected mass production and the consumer culture of the post-war years. But for many reasons, architecture does not always move forward in clear or linear ways. It may seem obvious that the same developments in materials and manufacturing techniques in homeware and electrical goods would be useful to architecture. And it might seem equally obvious that the relatively primitive technology of piling up lumps of fired clay or blocks of stone would be replaced by more modern materials and methods. But architecture is pulled in many directions, and material choices are not driven solely by technical requirements or economic factors or public taste or the desires of architects but by a complex intersection of all these things and more.

Paint

Is paint an architectural material? It carries no load, and it provides no support. You can't assemble it or make things from it. But it serves a functional purpose, protecting other materials from abrasion or weathering, and it can profoundly affect the appearance and character of buildings. Paint is a fantastic architectural material. It offers more bang for your buck than any other. It is transformative: its skin-deep surface not only covers a multitude of sins but also offers meaningful pleasures of colour, pattern and decoration.

This might sound more like do it yourself than architecture, the sort of thing people do to their own houses rather than something that architects are particularly interested in. But there are significant examples of great architecture that uses paint and painted surfaces for profound effect. The traditional domestic architecture of Tiébélé in Burkina Faso features richly symbolic painted surfaces. Using freehand painting as well as engravings and reliefs across the undulating surfaces of the mud-brick walls, this is an architecture of both space and surface, where the shape of the building interacts with a flexible symbolic layer. The decoration mixes abstract, geometric patterns with animist and celestial symbols that ripple across the imperfect surfaces.

Painting is used to spectacular effect in the church of Sant'Ignazio in Rome, where the ceiling frescoes create trompe l'oeil illusions of depth and projection. Painted over a fifteen-year period by Andrea Pozzo, the frescoes depict an architecture on top of the architecture. Columns, vaults, domes and arches project upwards in a dizzying vortex populated by figures and action. Paint both masks and extends the architecture, dissolving the actual surface in favour of an illusion of seemingly limitless space.

Paint – like many aspects of decoration and ornament – can be seen as a distraction in architecture, a superficial rather than a fundamental element. No doubt this has something to do its transience and impermanence. Paint does not always last. The richly painted, highly decorative surfaces of ancient Greek architecture went unknown for centuries, having long since been bleached away by the sun. When Le Corbusier photographed the Parthenon in Athens for his book *Towards a New Architecture* in 1927, he extolled the naked, unadorned beauty of its white marble surfaces. An entire theory of architecture emerged from this historic misreading, one that extolled the natural qualities of materials over the application of decoration or symbolism.

Before we leave this short plea to consider paint as an important material for architecture, we should look at one slightly more contemporary example. The post-war American architect Charles Moore was known for his exuberant, richly colourful work. Moore was a master of the domestic interior, a brilliant designer of houses where his playful sense of humour and profound appreciation of the richness of domestic life could find expression. The house he designed for himself in New Haven while dean of the School of Architecture at Yale University is a brilliant case in point. Moore bought a modest, nineteenth-century timber-framed house and turned its interior into an explosion of colour and pop art ornamentation. Moore painted surfaces in acidic pop colours and applied op art patterns and abstract graphics in a way that both highlighted the architecture and overrode it. His interior has some of the psychedelic qualities of the 1960s acid rock music that was contemporaneous with his design: it is a mind-expanding, consciousness-altering experience. Paint, here, is elevated to a role of profound architectural importance.

Timber

One of the emerging factors governing the choice of materials today is the amount of energy required to produce them. Brick and concrete, for instance, rely not only on the extraction of materials from the earth but also on carbon-intense methods of production. For this reason, there has been a return to one of architecture's oldest materials: timber. We will deal with timber's structural properties in the next chapter, so here we will focus on timber as cladding, timber as decoration and timber as detail.

Timber is abundant and renewable. It can be grown, cut and grown again. Trees provide oxygen and offer rich habitats for insects, birds and mammals. Timber offers an incredible flexibility as a building material. It can be cut into sections and used as structure, planed into panels and used as cladding and worked into complex extrusions or turned into decorative sections. It provides structure, decoration and detail, sometimes within the same component.

Timber shingles, for instance, form an outer layer to buildings, protecting them from rain and snow. Cut with curved or straight ends to each shingle, they offer delicate all-over pattern, too.

Russia's vast areas of forest, particularly in the north, meant that it developed a highly sophisticated timber-based architecture over many centuries. The wooden Orthodox churches built in the seventeenth and eighteenth centuries were glorious confections of steeply pitched roofs, bell towers and onion domes clad in complex jigsaws of shingles. Sometimes the churches grew successively larger elements: roofs on roofs and domes on domes like some fabulous fungal growth, spatial, structural and decorative at the same time. Later, in the nineteenth century, many of these churches were rebuilt more soberly in stone, but the ones that remain are some of the most remarkable timber structures ever built. At the same time, Russia's domestic architecture showed off the delicate patterns able to be carved in wood. The boards around windows and doors and the ends of gables and roof joists would all be carved with decorative fretwork.

The Swedish architect Erik Gunnar Asplund designed an exquisite timber building in Stockholm in 1920. The Woodland Chapel is in the Skogskyrkogården cemetery, part of a landscape populated by buildings designed by Asplund and his one-time partner, Sigurd Lewerentz. The chapel is a small rectangular structure located in a clearing among pine trees. It has a steeply pitched roof clad in timber shingles, supported at one end by a group of white-painted timber columns. The roof forms a dark canopy, and the columns have the character of trees so that we are invited to see this building almost as a continuation of the forest. It is simple and delicate but also beautifully balanced, a rustic temple. Later we will see how timber construction was translated into stone as part of the development of the classical language of architecture. In his little Stockholm cemetery chapel, Asplund reversed the direction of travel and made a perfect classical temple back into a perfectly realised timber shed.

The Spanish architectural practice TEd'A has updated several traditions of timber construction in its recent project for a new school in Orsonnens in Switzerland (fig. 24). Referencing Swiss chalet architecture, TEd'A's building is a large timber shed, formed by a timber frame and clad in super-sized planks cut to resemble enormous shingles. The internal structure uses glulam beams (sections of timber literally glued together to make them stronger). The resulting huge timber pieces of the main structure are contrasted with a more delicate wooden framework that forms the walls and roof supports. This is an unsentimental but immensely sophisticated rereading of historical building techniques where timber forms the structure, cladding and decoration, with elements ranging in scale from huge structural members to delicate filigree patterns.

Increasingly, timber is being looked at for large commercial office buildings as well as for housing and other typologies. New techniques such as cross-laminated timber panels that can be manufactured in factories and then quickly assembled on site increase

FIG. 24 School in Orsonnens, Fribourg, designed by TEd'A Arquitectes.

the material's potential. At the same time, timber's versatility means that it occurs throughout buildings in the form of linings and panelling, furniture and fittings. It can be used raw but also reconstituted into MDF boards and plywood sheets. It can be used to form decorative mouldings and ornamental surrounds and handrails. It is the support that holds buildings together, but it is also the stuff that we touch.

Architecture is the assembling of materials together to make buildings and spaces. The arrangement of materials, the way that they combine and form junctions, layers and systems, is a profound part of the pleasure of architecture. Material choices lead to stylistic decisions and spatial consequences, and they offer a form of composition in themselves. Materials are therefore impossible to separate from the other ways that we have looked at architecture so far. They are not an afterthought or a simple choice once the big decisions have been made, but a profound organising principle in themselves. They engage all the senses, from the visual pleasure of a patterned brick wall or the feel of a timber balustrade to the squeak of a floorboard or the smell of fresh paint.

CHAPTER 5

Structure

U NLIKE materials or style, but perhaps like space, structure is not always visible. Structure – understood literally – is the thing that holds a building up. It is made of something, comprising a material, or a set of materials, and so one might ask why I have separated the two here. The answer is that structure is as much a principle as a literal, physical element. Structures are made from physical matter, but they rely on the way that matter is used. The structure of a building is therefore not necessarily what you can see but what it is doing. It is the product of forces and loads and calculations, and so although it comprises physical stuff it dictates how the whole building behaves and how everything stays in one place.

It is also the bit that the architect doesn't design. It is generally understood that architects design buildings and that structural engineers design structures. But the relationship between the two is complex and overlapping and not always clearly authored. The architect might come up with a structural idea, a principle of how the building stands up, but it is the engineer who designs this component. Sometimes the architect might have little interest in structure and sometimes the engineer might introduce a structural idea that changes the course of the design and profoundly affects the result. Structure can be a pragmatic response to requirements – a simple and expedient way to hold things up – or it can be an innovative and dynamic driver of the shape a building takes.

The structural system effects much more than the stability of a building, its ability to stand up: it dictates how tall or wide it is, how open or cellular, the size of the spaces within, as well as their character, informing – for instance – the ratio of solid wall to glazed opening or whether a room has columns in. Structure is the inner order of a building, the thing that holds it all together. It is a principle and a fact, and it is present as an underlying organisation. It is both extremely pragmatic and intensely profound.

It is also a metaphor for how many, many things – arguments, organisations, books, songs – are organised. We might talk about the structure of a piece of music or the plot structure of a film. Families have structure, as do offices and events. We talk about the structure of our lives or bemoan the fact that our days are too unstructured. We also use specific aspects of structure to describe how things other than buildings work. We might for instance talk about the foundations of an argument or a dispute. We might say that one person is carrying most of the load in a specific situation or that another is not offering enough support. Structure in this sense describes the essence and the underlying organisation of people, objects and things, as well as how people and things behave. Even to describe something as underlying is to adopt – on some level – a metaphor rooted in structure. When things are superficial or disconnected from their core we might describe them as a façade, something added to but not intrinsic to their structure.

So structure is profoundly bound up with how we think and how we conceive of relationships, whether they are the relationships between people and organisations or between objects and materials. It is the latter that concerns us here, but it is not possible to talk about structure without first understanding it as something more than the way buildings are made to stand up. In architectural terms it is as profound as composition and style in forming the character and organisation of a building, although it is also the bit that architects talk about the least. It is – remarkably, given its profound importance – often ignored in a lot of conversations about architecture. The structure of a building affects our understanding of it. Pertinently for this book, which is neither a history of architecture nor a construction handbook, it changes the way we experience buildings, and it shapes our interaction with them.

Load-Bearing Walls

We have already observed that structure is both visible and invisible, a physical presence as well as an underlying set of principles. How do we learn to understand structure – how a building stands up – at least on a basic, observational level? We can start with some simple structural principles and the differences between, say, buildings that use load-bearing walls and buildings that use frames. There are lots of other different types of structure – tensile structures, shell vaults, inflatable structures – but this first distinction feels like a useful starting point to establish some principles, a structure that we can use to understand structure.

Let's take a 'traditional' building, in this instance an ordinary terraced house of the type that would have been built in its thousands across the UK in the nineteenth century. This kind of building uses the walls as structure. The external walls are made of bricks, which are piled up, one on top of the other, to hold themselves up. A brick wall is its own structure. If it is very tall it might need buttressing – diagonal piers of brick that lean up against it. Or it might need to change direction in order to gain stability – long lines of brick wall are prone to falling over. But the structural principle of a brick wall is easy to grasp.

Buildings are not only formed of walls, so the brick also needs to support floors. Traditionally these would have been made of wood, long sections of timber laid horizontally and supported at the sides on the brick walls. Walls need foundations and these were achieved by corbelling the bricks – that is, increasing the width of the wall by pushing each successive course of brick out further than the last. This happens below the ground, so the bricks step out to form something like a foot that spreads the load. The timber floor joists help to hold the walls together, bracing what might otherwise be unstable structures. Where there are windows, a structural lintel is required to span across the opening and support the bricks above it. Traditionally this is done by forming an arch with the brick, either flat or curving, with the bricks cut so that they slot in together, fanning out to form a self-supporting structure.

The roof is formed from a timber truss, a series of timbers fixed together to form a triangular web that spans across the width of the house and creates a sloped surface for the roof to shed rainwater. In a terrace, these roofs are lined up together with drainage running between. Typically, the front, street-facing wall will extend up higher than the roof to form a flat 'parapet' to unite all the houses together. Expediently, in this system, two houses will share the same wall, meaning fewer walls to build overall, and the terracing provides an overall stability to the whole.

So we have a very simple structural principle established: load-bearing masonry walls with timber floors. The size of the houses can vary, as can windows and doors. Different bricks can be used, or the bricks can be faced or entirely replaced with stone. Houses can be grander or more elaborate without changing the principle of their construction. Most of Georgian and Victorian London was built this way. Stand in one of London's Georgian squares and you can see a simple scaling up from the single lump of fired clay that is a brick to whole streets of houses. We can see the materials that make up these buildings, but we can also understand the structural principle that combines them into a coherent system.

The evolution of this system produced much of the architecture of eighteenth- and nineteenth-century London, a whole recipe book of brick details and window designs, doorcases and other embellishments that added refinement or specific character to an otherwise relatively standardised product. The efficiency of it lay in its reproducibility. Sometimes the steepness of the topography proved a challenge, but it was an efficient way to build the same product repeatedly.

Here we can see a marriage between materials – what a building is made of – and its structure – how these materials work. Clearly some of the materials, such as the elaborate timber and plaster surrounds that lent importance to front doors or windows, are not part of the structure. But they are enabled by its simplicity, a way to adorn straightforward stretches of brick wall. What's more, the materials involved are being used in very straightforward ways that can be understood in principle without complex physics being involved. We can imagine the distribution of loads, the way that forces generally push down and outwards, and therefore we understand the structure.

Frames

Although one might associate structural frames with contemporary buildings – skyscrapers and office blocks using steel and concrete – it is a very old way to build. We have already seen that some buildings that look like they are made of brick are constructed using timber frames. Medieval buildings in the UK were often made of frames because timber was plentiful. It is easy to use and can be cut and planed and made to fit together in ways that precise materials such as steel cannot. A sixteenth-century timber-framed house is not in effect that different from one made of brick. The walls are still the structure, though they are made of bits of wood rather than lumps of clay and will therefore feel a bit different and sound different when you tap them.

Timber frames of this type can be covered in anything – brick, stone, plaster, weatherboarding. Sometimes the frame is infilled rather than covered up, and this gives rise to a very distinctive 'half-timbered' style. When people refer to 'mock-Tudor' as an architectural style they generally mean modern buildings that imitate half-timbering. This is interesting not only in terms of how a structural principle can become a style of architecture but also how that style can then evolve into something else entirely. The contemporary mock-Tudor house uses timbers as a decorative feature, an element added often to load-bearing walls to make a house look as if it is made of timber. It is more complicated than that, because the timbers make no plausible attempt to appear structural – several centuries of derivations of timber-framing have meant that we often divorce the appearance of timber from any structural role.

Origin Myths

Mock-timber construction is the first time in this chapter that we have encountered the issue of architectural style making structure symbolic rather than literal. We have separated timber-frame structures from masonry (brick and stone) ones because that seems a straightforward and simple way to start talking about structure, but it is important to note too that things are not quite that simple. Structure is also about representation: that is to say, it is about what it represents – speaks about – as much as what it does.

In architectural theory, timber construction is often considered to be the beginning of architecture. Many architectural theorists and writers – from the Roman architect Vitruvius to the twentieth-century modernist Le Corbusier – have speculated on the origins of architecture, which is to say the origins of the classical language of architecture. One of the most famous drawings to speculate on this adorned the front of a book called *Essay on Architecture*, published in 1753 and written by Marc-Antoine Laugier. The drawing – by Charles-Dominique-Joseph Eisen – depicts a myth of the first piece of architecture, a primitive hut, constructed from timber and arranged to form a simple house shape. It is a frame structure using raw, unplaned timber, tree trunks and branches that have been picked up from the forest floor and assembled into a small building – a temple – that appears to be still half-growing, with leaves and branches sprouting from its roof.

Laugier goes on to explain how each piece of timber became translated into the elements of classical architecture: the tree trunks that form the vertical elements became classical columns, the roots their bases and the branches their capitals. Every element of classical architecture and its assemblage of decorative elements is accounted for by original timber elements. The ends of the timber joists laid flat to form floors became the dentil courses – the row of tooth-like notches – of a classical entablature, for example.

The veracity of these myths of architectural theory is ultimately less important than their effect on what architects do. There is an intertwining of timber construction and masonry construction, and one often imitates the other. Laugier speculated that the language of stone construction is really a system of symbolic elements translated from elemental timber construction. Contemporary houses that appear to have timber frames – or at least make the vaguest of allusions to having a timber frame – are made of bricks, or blocks.

There is a point here: things are not always as they seem, and what appears to be structural sometimes isn't. The reasons why architects or designers might want to suggest that a building is made from something when it is made from something else are complex, and partially addressed in the previous chapter. In a book dedicated to how we read and understand the buildings around us, the literalness of what we look at is important. So we will return to the issue of real and fake structure – and some points between – after we have hopefully established some more principles about it.

The Dom-Ino Frame

Le Corbusier's 1914 drawing of the Dom-Ino frame is another origin myth of architecture (fig. 25). The image appears in Corbusier's book *Towards a New Architecture*, a modernist polemic in which he sets out his five principles of modern architecture. The Dom-Ino frame illustrates these principles and its rests on a structural system.

The drawing – really a diagram – shows a framed structure where the floors are supported by columns. The columns form a grid of supports unconnected to the external walls, so the building's structure is self-supporting and independent of its enclosing walls.

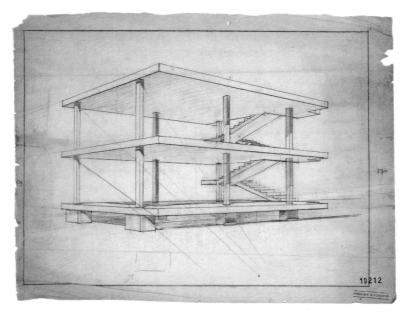

FIG. 25 Maison Dom-Ino, designed by Le Corbusier.

These are free to be designed as the architect wishes. They can be fully glazed, infilled with panels, built up with brick or block or a smaller sub-frame of their own. Internal walls are similarly free to be placed wherever. Free of the need to hold anything up, walls become expressive elements able to distribute space according to the architect's wish.

Various other things come from this principle. The roof is flat, which means it can be occupied as a roof garden or terrace. The walls don't need to go down to the ground, which means that the ground floor itself can be open, with the building suspended above. External walls can be completely glazed, or not, depending on the architect's wish. It sounds appealing – liberating, even. No more chunks of heavy stone. No more gloomy basements or uninhabitable lofts, just lots of space stretching out before us. Sun, air, views: a gravity-defying lightness of being.

Understood in this way, the evolution of twentieth-century buildings seems much clearer. All those apartment blocks with their open ground floors, and access decks hoisted up in the sky above us. Skyscrapers with their columns of glass stretching up into the sky. Windows are not holes seemingly punched into a stone or brick wall but more like a curtain hanging from a skeletal structure within.

Le Corbusier's drawing is of a concrete structure, though the principle would be the same if the elements were made of steel. Concrete, steel and – to a lesser extent – timber can act in ways that brick and stone can't. They can be cantilevered – that is, they can extend out horizontally or vertically beyond their point of support. A steel beam can project beyond the steel column that supports it, which makes the external face of the building something different from the structure that supports it.

Concrete is a remarkable material which I have talked about in the previous chapter. It is a semi-liquid substance that can be poured into different shapes and frozen into plastic forms. It can be sculpted like clay, and it is incredibly hard and durable. To form projections and cantilevers it requires a steel mesh – called reinforcement – which allows it to appear to defy gravity and hang in mid-air. No wonder architects love it. It allows an extraordinary range of options and for buildings to do remarkable things.

Let's look at one of Le Corbusier's most famous buildings as an example. We encountered this building before, when it was used to illustrate different spatial concepts in the book *Collage City* (fig. 16). We are interested here, though, in the structural principles that underlie the architecture. The Unité de Habitation is a block of 337 flats in Marseille, France. It was built between 1947 and 1953 and was the first of several similar blocks designed by Le Corbusier that represented a refined development of the principles set out in his Dom-Ino House of 1914. The building has a concrete frame, expressed on the outside as an open grid that defines each apartment. True to his five principles, the ground floor is largely open, populated by stairs and lift shafts allowing access to the apartments above. The legs of his concrete frame are freely expressed as monumental columns, like a giant's feet. The roof is flat but populated by expressive sculptural elements such as exhaust vents and extravagant sunshades. There is also a small nursery school and a swimming pool, both of which have dramatic views of the Mediterranean and the hills that surround Marseille.

It is easy to sound like a modernist proselytiser here, regurgitating Le Corbusier's own words. We have already touched on the myths of classical architecture, and here are the myths of modernism. Le Corbusier contrasted his Dom-Ino House with Laugier's primitive hut. Concrete is the origin myth of modern architecture.

The Rise and Rise of the Steel Frame

Concrete and steel frames changed the game, allowing architecture to do things it hadn't before. But these materials were also used by architects keen to do the opposite: to make architecture look or refer to how it *had* been done before. The advent of the steel frame allowed buildings to grow higher – much higher than masonry construction will allow. This creates another issue, which is: if an architect still wants to use or refer to the classical language, how do they do it?

To explore this intersection of material, structure and style, let's look at examples in both London and New York. Two technical developments prefigured the growth of the skyscraper: steel frames and elevators. Arguably it is the elevator that is more significant in allowing the building of multi-floored structures, but they would not have been possible without the steel frame either. Concrete can do the same job, but it becomes increasingly heavy and is slower to build. Forming concrete at great heights involves a lot more people and takes a lot more time.

So the steel frame was the dominant structure for the commercial buildings that developed in the latter years of the nineteenth century, especially in the USA. Steel also began to affect the design of smaller commercial buildings in other cities. We will start with one in London.

The former Royal Insurance building on the corner of Piccadilly and St James's Street is a remarkable and daring building designed at the start of the twentieth century and completed in 1907. It is classically detailed, with a steel frame. Its designers – J.J. Joass and John Belcher – revelled in the freedom that resulted, stretching the classical language of columns, entablatures and mouldings across the face of a structure that bears little relationship to classical proportions or harmonies. Everything appears stretched, almost to breaking point. It is as if a crocheted cover has been pulled over an object much larger than it was meant to be. That sounds slightly disastrous, but the skill and imagination of the architects has allowed a reinvention of the language used, an innovative and remarkable example of something settled and ordered becoming dynamic and in flux.

Joass and Belcher's building has been described as mannerist, the style of architecture developed in the late Renaissance inspired by Michelangelo that played violent and disruptive games with the classical language. At St James's Street, this reinvention occurs as a direct result of the advent of the steel frame and the application of classical detailing to buildings of very different shapes and proportions than their classical antecedents. Something similar but on a vastly larger scale happened in North American cities around the same period.

The Guaranty Building in Buffalo, New York was one of the first commercial skyscrapers in the world. It was designed by the American architectural practice Sullivan and Adler and completed in 1896 (fig. 26). It is a comparatively modest twelve storeys and

FIG. 26 Guaranty Building, Buffalo, New York, designed by Louis Sullivan.

has an iron frame as its principal structure. What is principally interesting about the building – and others by its designer Louis Sullivan – is the way the classical language of architecture has been manipulated to work with the new construction system. Formally, it is like a stretched Italian palazzo, pulled upwards from three or four to twelve storeys. Like a classical building its vertical form is broken into a base and a superstructure, which is to say that the ground-floor storey is separated from the upper floors by a horizontal shift in material. At the top, the building's eaves curve outward to form something like the capital of a classical column. In fact, the building – like many early skyscrapers – can be seen as an enormous, inhabited classical column.

But Sullivan does something else, which is to adorn the building in rich terracotta faience. From a distance, the Guaranty Building looks relatively simple – sober, even. Up close, though, it is consumed by a kind of architectural foliage, a rampant ivy-like growth that covers every surface. The decoration has connections to European art nouveau, the kind of etiolated and exaggerated floral motifs seen in buildings in cities like Vienna at the turn of the century. But Sullivan's delicate and complex web of ornament has been developed here to cover a large commercial skyscraper. The result is paradoxical and contradictory, something both muscular and fragile-looking.

Sullivan designed several important commercial buildings following the Guaranty in Buffalo, in cities such as Chicago and New York. He defined much of the form of the early skyscraper and demonstrated how classical architectural detailing could be applied to this entirely new typology. The vertical grid of space formed by the iron or steel structure brought with it an entirely new type of architecture. Sullivan's work bridged a gap: it tried to retain aspects of an older, load-bearing architecture in an era of steel frames. In doing so he invented something else, something strange and very beautiful.

Skyscrapers and commercial offices would abandon this line of enquiry for the most part, developing an architectural language that grew more naturally from the demands and opportunities of frame structures and high-rise buildings. In a sense, Sullivan attempted the impossible, trying to contain an object that is endless and endlessly repetitive within an aesthetic system that is about limits and articulating differences. But architecture has always done this, evolving answers to emerging requirements and new forms of building. For most of the twentieth century, New York defined the idea of the contemporary city, the skyscraper representing both extreme bureaucracy – identical offices or apartments piled up on top of each other – and rapacious capital – the maximisation of profit. This was enabled in a very direct way by the development of the iron-and-steel frame.

Structure does not always act so directly or obviously in the formation of architecture. We have looked at simple distinctions between load-bearing and framed structures and how each develops and defines different kinds of architecture. Both – in their different ways – result in an architecture that is massive, physically impressive and permanent. So let's look at structures that define themselves through lightness and aspire to temporality and ideas of change and flexibility.

Tensile Structures

Pneumatic and tensile structures represent a form of anti-archi-tecture. If architecture has defined itself historically as something that aspires to permanence and strength, tensile structures do the opposite, aiming for a more ethereal presence and the potential to change. We are familiar with pneumatic structures: they appear at children's parties as bouncy castles and as inflatable mattresses. Surely these objects have no more than a passing relationship to architecture, being more like cartoonish depictions of buildings than actual inhabitable ones. And it is true that there is an essential, practical problem with inflatables in that the interior space is filled with air, rather than, say, people.

So inflatable architecture can be sculptural and physical, and it can look like a building – in an exaggerated and slightly bizarre sense – but it is hard to get into, literally speaking. The English high-tech architect Norman Foster developed numerous innovative buildings in the 1960s and 1970s, several of which attempted to escape the traditional structures and materials of architecture. He looked for novel construction techniques that would allow buildings to be built with greater speed and efficiency than traditional ones. For Foster – at least at that point in his career – temporariness, cheapness and lightness were virtues to aspire to.

Perhaps the ultimate expression of this was a relatively modest office building designed in Hemel Hempstead, a New Town on the edge of London, in 1970. The office was for a company called Computer Technology and it was roughly 8,000 square feet in size. What was unique about it was that the office was housed in an inflatable, vaulted structure. Foster got around the main problem with inflatables by making the exterior envelope the inflatable part, which then enclosed an inhabitable interior space. This envelope had a double thickness and the space between was filled with air. It resembled a very large, long tent where the canvas sides were inflated. It took just fifty-five minutes to put up. It is not recorded how long it lasted, but contemporary photographs make it look more civilised than it sounds, kitted out with desks, pot plants and flexible overhead lighting cleverly sewn into the plastic lining.

Foster's temporary office appears now as very much a product of the early 1970s, unconcerned with energy prices and in love with technology as a driver and liberator of society. Foster was drawing on alternative industrial techniques to develop an architecture that was lightweight, modular, moveable and product-based. But his work was not unprecedented. Other architects of the time were interested in similar technologies, although sometimes with different end games in mind. The anarchic Austrian group Haus-Rucker-Co made a series of inflatable and pneumatic structures in the late 1960s and early 1970s, but instead of deploying these in the service of corporate clients – as Foster did – they were interested in their mind-altering properties. Mirroring the psychedelic impulse of the counterculture, Haus-Rucker-Co constructed immersive environments that played with perception and behaviour. The best known of these works was perhaps Oasis No. 7 of 1972, a plastic bubble popping out of the gallery in which it was sited, as if it had been inflated from within (fig. 27). Inside it was a little platform and a palm tree, an alternative utopic environment attempting to float free of architecture.

More obviously, Foster drew on the extraordinary innovations of an American architect and inventor called Buckminster Fuller.

FIG. 27   Oasis No. 7, Kassel, designed by Haus-Rucker-Co.

Fuller was fascinated by efficiency and mass production and by the idea that architecture could become more like a machine, a sophisticated piece of technological equipment rather than all those ancient stuffy things made of stone and brick. He wanted to capture the opportunities of mass production, factory repetition and Fordist efficiency. Famously, Fuller once asked a client how much they wanted their house to weigh. He invented something called the Dymaxion House, which was a very early form of flat-pack, kit-of-parts construction. He also developed a design for the Dymaxion car, an odd, sci-fi-looking vehicle that Foster would eventually have built as a tribute to his hero, albeit as a one-off prototype rather than the mass-produced version of Fuller's dreams.

Fuller was also obsessed with domes. Specifically, he developed a dome formed by a network of triangular frames. Known as a geodesic structure, it was a highly efficient way to create a spherical enclosure. Fuller built a number of these, collaborating with the US military, who were interested in the possibilities of construct-ing instant enclosures that could be flown or helicoptered into the battlefield. Fuller also lived in one, and a set of fascinating photo-graphs shows him and his wife at home in their dome in the 1950s; their oddly traditional wooden furniture and Eisenhower-era hair-cuts sit in defiance of the sci-fi environment.

Fuller's ideas for domes got bigger and more ambitious, even-tually culminating in a proposal to cover Manhattan – and all its skyscrapers – with one vast bubble. He dreamt of a technologically driven architecture that would free itself of its burdensome heritage in order to better answer society's problems. Sometimes – as in the Manhattan dome – he answered questions that nobody had asked. But his pioneering work points to a very different concept of architecture, one in which structure and technology are everything.

We might ask what this means in a book devoted to the every-day experience of architecture. How do these largely academic exercises help us to enjoy architecture? Are we likely to come across actual examples? Well, yes: if not in galleries that still exhibit Haus-Rucker-Co's experiments then in entertainment structures and temporary stages of music and other events. There are more permanent examples, too. The 1972 Olympic Games were held in Munich and located in an area of the city that had been flattened by bombing in the Second World War (fig. 28). Rather than clear the site of bomb damage, the site's master planner Frei Otto instead sculpted the debris into a rolling landscape, an exaggerated artificial topography in which the main stadium and swimming pool were located. To enclose them, Otto designed a series of giant tensile structures, tents made from interlocking acrylic panels held up by a complex network of cables. The tents resemble a crystalline mountain range dancing across an artificial valley. Otto dispensed with architecture in the conventional sense and invented a hybrid landscape inhabited by lightweight enclosures. We could see this either as architecture without structure, or as architecture that is all structure. Otto's cobweb of cables and transparent panels is both structure and enclosure, a building where the elements holding it up are also the elements enclosing and defining space.

In his Munich work Otto realised some of Fuller's ideas, the most fundamental of which involved the negation of architecture itself, at least in the conventional sense. Sometimes, though, architecture strikes back, reclaiming structure for itself. I will finish this chapter with the work of Kazuo Shinohara, a highly influential Japanese architect who died in 2006. Shinohara's work went through several phases but almost all his buildings are characterised by the surprising and sometimes awkward presence of structure. It is there in his Tanakawa House, where a series of timber supports marches across the main space, and it is there in House on a Curved Road, where the timber columns become concrete and dominate the interior. It is also very much there in his House in Uehara, where the concrete columns become massive tree-like objects planted incongruously in the living space (fig. 29).

FIG. 28 Olympic Stadium, Munich, designed by Frei Otto.

FIG. 29 Interior view of the House in Uehara, designed by Kazuo Shinohara.

Looking at these spaces, an obvious question arises: why would an architect place such cumbersome objects where they are least wanted? What practical reason could there be for expressing the structure in such a way that it inhibited the use of the space it was supposedly supporting? What kind of architect does this, and why? Shinohara does what I started off this chapter by denying. He makes structure visible. He gives it physical form, but he also exaggerates it, expresses the forces holding the building up and places them in full view. Structure is not the only thing happening in his houses, but he gives it a presence. It is not an invisible agent nor a conceptual principle nor a set of calculations hidden away somewhere. It is a physical experience.

Revealingly, Shinohara originally trained as a mathematician. His work is precise and meticulous but also highly cerebral. The insistent presence of structure in his work is like the engineer's calculations taking centre stage, literally becoming material. Structure in his work becomes the architecture, not in a practical sense but in the sense of its previously invisible principles becoming the stuff that we experience – perhaps, even, the part we can enjoy the most.

CHAPTER 6

Use

ARCHITECTS have many different words for use: programme, brief, function, even typology. But this chapter is called use because that feels closest to how we might think about buildings when we try to understand them. We are the users, after all.

All buildings have a use. Unlike other art forms, architecture is almost always commissioned to serve a use. How does this use affect the way it has been designed? How much of architecture is given over to use? Is use an inconvenience, an excuse to build but not the point of building? Does architecture exist independently of the mundane or practical demands required of it? Is architecture the elegant, beautiful way of making a building useful? Or is it the bit added on after use has been catered for? Is architecture useful? Or does it get in the way of making decent, functional buildings, an unnecessary frill or a designer's conceit?

An account of architecture via style, composition, space, materials and structure – the ways that we have looked at buildings so far – doesn't account for what they are used for. Use has come up, but it has been incidental to our main focus. There are overlaps and relationships between style and use, composition and function. But the same style of architecture can be applied to very different buildings. Take neo-Georgian, which we looked at in Chapter 1. It was used for large institutional buildings such as museums, schools and galleries but also for houses, churches and even factories. Modernism was not so much a style as a fundamental shift of approach, but it wasn't limited to specific uses and was applied to all building types.

Use seems to have little to do with stylistic categories. Composition might come closer, because the use of buildings clearly affects the way that they are spatially organised. But uses can also change, and buildings intended for one function can be adapted to suit another, so a question around use might be: how much does it dictate the design of a building? The answer to this might vary. A church is a building with a very specific composition linked to precise ceremonies and traditions. An office building offers more generic space, less defined by use.

Use is oddly rather marginal to histories of architecture. These mostly look at buildings in terms of evolutions of style, through the work of single architects or via specific historic periods. Use tends to be secondary or regarded as a slight backwater to the major events and shifts in architectural history. Think of a typical monograph on a famous architect. Let's take the Indian architect B.V. Doshi, whose work we will look at in more detail later in the chapter. Doshi designed schools, houses, art galleries and cultural buildings, mostly in his native India. But books on his work tend to focus on the evolution of his personal architecture, its influences and stylistic shifts over the period of his working life. Use is secondary to something less tangible but seemingly more important to do with architecture.

Beauty and Utility

> Have nothing in your house that you do not know to be beautiful or believe to be useful.

These words were spoken by the writer and designer William Morris in a lecture given at the Birmingham School of Design in 1880. Morris makes a distinction between beauty and use, aesthetics and utility. He doesn't say that beautiful objects can't be useful, but he suggests that they aren't the same thing. Use exists regardless of beauty, and vice versa.

A popular conception of the art of architecture might have it that creativity lies at the opposite end of a sliding scale from practical requirements. Beauty is one thing, usefulness another. We might describe a boring or uninspiring building as 'purely functional', as if no other considerations had gone into its design. This assumes that a functional or useful thing is necessarily lacking in beauty or other qualities. In claiming something as merely functional, or merely useful, we are clearly identifying a lack. Usefulness without beauty is uninspiring – ugly, even.

Some of this stems from the modern movement and that tendency within it that was known as functionalism. So when someone says that they don't like a building because it is merely functional, they might mean that they don't like modernist buildings. They might be bemoaning what they see as a more general lack of beauty in modern buildings, a tendency within contemporary architecture to attach value only to ideas of utility.

There is a sense here that for buildings to be beautiful or elegant or inspiring or even successful they need to transcend their use or their function. Use is assumed as a given, a baseline, something that all buildings have. Here is another quote, this time from the architecture critic and writer Nikolaus Pevsner. At the start of his book *An Outline of European Architecture* (first published in 1943), Pevsner states: 'A bicycle shed is a building. Lincoln Cathedral is a piece of architecture.'

It is the first line of the book. It sets out Pevsner's entire conception of architecture in essence. And it equates beauty not with use but with status and grandeur. Pevsner doesn't say which bicycle shed, but he is quite specific about the cathedral. We can also infer that while the former is ordinary and mundane and *merely useful*, the latter belongs to architecture and to art. Pevsner might have useful things in his house, but – unlike Morris – he accords them a lower status than the beautiful things.

Pevsner's distinction is problematic for several reasons, but underlying it is a sense that use – however well accommodated – is not sufficient to make architecture. It might even be a drag on it. He also suggests that there is a hierarchy of use and that perhaps the more obviously useful a building is (in the practical sense), the less it can aspire to be architecture. Use lies at the other end of the spectrum from beauty.

So use is problematic in architecture. One might almost consider it architecture's guilty secret, a slight embarrassment for an activity that aspires to the status of art but is all too often dragged down by use. And yet it is the reason why architecture exists. Without a need, without functional necessity – however loosely defined – architecture would not just be useless, it would also cease to be. Who commissions a building without use? We need to find some buildings where use is considered more than an inconvenience, where architecture comes directly out of its use.

Can we ascribe architectural qualities to use, assess it in ways that have meaning beyond the practical? How do we frame the practical as something more profound? When something works well, when it doesn't simply do what it is supposed to but does it in a way that somehow embodies and frames and expresses that use, it can be profound. Examples of this might come from both humble sources (a bicycle shed) or grander and more important ones, too (Lincoln Cathedral). In this sense, they aren't different.

All buildings have a use: cathedrals and bicycle sheds and lots of other things besides: petrol stations, art galleries, schools, prisons, shopping malls, electricity sub-stations, club houses, post offices and town halls. To a greater or lesser degree some of these building uses summon up clear and relatively unambiguous images. A petrol station, for instance, might generally consist of a large, horizontal awning held up on columns and with a small shed or pavilion underneath it. We recognise the relationships between use and form here: the pumps are under the awning, which protects us from rain while we fill the car up with petrol. We pay for the petrol in the little shed, which is also a shop where we can buy other things.

Most petrol stations, with some variations, look like this. They are use translated into architecture – or at least building. Their use does not stop them from being beautiful. If you drive through Copenhagen, I can recommend filling up at Arne Jacobsen's Skovshoved petrol station which is both starkly beautiful and highly functional. Its awning is like an elegant, slender mushroom and the shop is clad in pristine and glistening white ceramic tiles.

It is possible to find ordinary petrol stations beautiful, too. The American pop artist Ed Ruscha collected photographs of them together in his 1963 artwork *Twentysix Gasoline Stations*. Ruscha likes ordinary things, but he sees in them something beautiful – not perhaps in their architecture, exactly, but in both their familiarity and their sameness. I feel the same way. They have an eerie elegance at night, when their neon lights shine out of the inky blackness.

So we can find ordinary, useful things beautiful. But can we make usefulness itself beautiful? Can usefulness be the defining character of architecture? How does use shape a building? The Roger Stevens Building on Leeds University campus was designed in 1970 by the British architecture firm Chamberlin, Powell and Bon. More famous for designing the Barbican Estate in London, Chamberlin, Powell and Bon were also responsible for several university buildings in the post-war period. They masterplanned the expansion of the University of Leeds campus and the Roger Stevens Building is the standout piece of architecture within it.

Apart from being a remarkable and sculpturally audacious work, the Roger Stevens Building tells us something very interesting about use and how it can be articulated as architecture. The building is essentially an auditorium – a lecture hall – a fact that is expressed on the outside, as it was in many university buildings in the 1950s and 1960s, by an elevation that steps up in line with the rake of the interior seating. But something more profound and original happens on the inside. The rake of the lecture hall seating continues into the staircase that accesses it. Doors into the lecture hall open directly onto the stairs, so that every few steps you can slide into it at a different seating level. It is as if there is one vast staircase separated by a wall so that one side is a lecture hall and the other is circulation and access. Instead of filing into the hall through one door and climbing up a stair to find a row to sit in, you enter the room at different levels.

It is at once an incredibly simple and direct idea and a rather complicated one. It is not as practical as one might hope. There is a slight confusion in which door to use and a certain amount of awkward filing in and out. To be fair, it results in a similar level of confusion to that encountered in any form of auditorium when people need to negotiate each other, the sort of kerfuffle that occurs when one person arrives in a cinema late for the screening, requiring everyone else in their row to stand up awkwardly to let them past. But the functionality is ultimately less interesting to consider here than the way that the building expresses it, is built around, this function. It articulates its use through a very direct spatial arrangement that *feels* incredibly functional even if it isn't quite. The building *is* its use in a way that is very direct but also very expressive. You can see what it does on the outside and feel what it does on the inside.

The Architecture of Use

'Form follows function' was a mantra of twentieth-century modernism, though the phrase was coined by Louis Sullivan in the late nineteenth century. As we saw in the previous chapter, Sullivan was wrestling with the emerging model of the skyscraper and the advent of steel-frame technology, both of which he thought would develop into a new kind of architecture.

Arguably, though, it was in the eighteenth century when the concept of a building as a rational expression of its use emerged in earnest. The social reformer Jeremy Bentham developed his ideas for the panoptic prison in the 1790s. Panoptic means 'all-seeing' and Bentham's concept was for a prison based on the comprehensive surveillance of prisoners. The Panopticon – as it became known – is a circular prison with cells arranged to fan out around a central watchhouse. The layout enables the guards to see every prisoner.

Bentham's concept drew on theories for other emerging uses such as factories and schools, but it made use the single most powerful driver of the architectural form. The resulting design – the Panopticon was an unrealised concept – is closer to an industrial invention than a conventional piece of architecture: a functional machine. Its use – the incarceration and surveillance of prisoners – shaped the form of the building in a direct and unambiguous fashion. The Panopticon was intended as a machine of surveillance in much the same way that an engine is a machine for propelling a car. It is an extreme way to think about use in architecture, but it is a useful one. The Panopticon was a response to a perceived need, a building invented to address emerging ideas about prison and criminal reform. Bentham did not invent the use, but he invented a building that attempted to perfect it.

Bentham was a social reformer who saw buildings in much the same way that he saw legal and political reforms: as something that could be instrumentalised towards the social betterment of society. He was not particularly interested in architecture per se, and he certainly wasn't interested in the beauty part of William Morris's equation. The style of the architecture was of little use to him, and his invention would continue to influence the design of prisons long into the twentieth century. The neo-classical form taken by illustrations of Bentham's Panopticon was mostly irrelevant to him, though the style would become associated with the emerging industrial uses of the eighteenth and nineteenth centuries.

The industrial villages and idealised communities envisaged by the French neo-rationalist architect Claude-Nicolas Ledoux are a case in point. Ledoux was interested in the relationship of architecture and social reform too, and his buildings exemplified a supposedly rationalist view of behaviour and organisation. They embodied their use in much the same way as the Panopticon, becoming in effect machines for the rational organisation of society. The range of functions and uses addressed by Ledoux was wide and surprising. Few areas of human activity escaped his attention. His House of Pleasure was a design for a brothel within the ideal city of Choux. Designed in 1804, the building attempted to give form to a desire to reform and regulate prostitution. Looked at in perspective, the building is innocuous enough, an exercise in neo-classicism. The plan, though, is based on a phallus. Bedrooms are arranged along the shaft, which terminates in the semi-circular 'salon'. Sexual desire is clearly recognised here as exclusively male, but the point for us is the mechanised relationship between form and use. The House of Pleasure – which appears to be anything but – represents both male desire and its control via architecture.

The Use of Architecture

The late architectural historian Robin Evans wrote about Jeremy Bentham and the invention of the Panoptic prison in a book entitled *The Fabrication of Virtue*. Evans was interested in the relationship of buildings to social behaviour, and he explored this in other areas of design, too. In the late 1970s he wrote an influential essay entitled 'Figures, Doors and Passages' in which he traced the development of the corridor in domestic architecture. Evans explored a link between how houses are organised and how the life within them is organised, how their layouts shape our lives.

We have already looked at the work of Andrea Palladio and at the villas he built in the sixteenth century. In his essay, Evans notes that these villas contain no corridors and that, consequently, rooms are interconnected. To get to one room you must pass through another. More than that, the principal rooms tended to have little difference in function. They could, in effect, be used for different things depending on how furniture was arranged or who was in them.

This idea of a loose fit between spaces and their use is quite different from the contemporary Western home with its clear functions. It might seem obvious that houses should be made up of rooms with different uses – bathroom, kitchen, bedroom, etc. – but it has not always been this way. Evans traces the development of single uses for different rooms as a way of describing other things, such as emerging ideas of privacy and the separation of genders and ages within the home. Children's bedrooms, master bedrooms, playrooms, studies and other rooms with specifically coded uses do not necessarily change the architecture in stylistic terms, but they affect how we live and how we relate to each other. We might think these separations of use natural, but they profoundly influence our lives.

Of course, not all houses follow the same rules. Even within conservative societies, exceptions from these norms exist. A La Ronde is an eccentric house that overlooks the mouth of the River Axe in Devon (fig. 30). It is almost, but not quite, circular, a sixteen-sided rustic cottage with a large, conical roof split by dormer windows and surmounted by what looks like a kind of crow's nest or lookout point. Internally the house is no less strange: a central sixteen-sided hallway is surrounded by walls like a clockface.

FIG. 30 The Octagon at A La Ronde, Exmouth, designed by Jane and Mary Parminter.

A La Ronde was designed and built by two cousins, Mary and Jane Parminter. The cousins lived in the house together and the interior reflected their interests and their routines. The rooms were occupied to reflect the position of the sun as it passed around the house and the women would move furniture and function to suit. The Parminter cousins designed a house that dictated the routines of their day, the interior forming a chronological perambulatory circumnavigation. A La Ronde is not so much a house as a machine for experiencing domestic life. It is defined by use, but in ways that are about experience much more than utility.

A La Ronde bears a superficial resemblance to Bentham's Panopticon. Both are circular and have the character of a machine, or an invention. In Bentham's case it is a machine of surveillance, while in the Parminters', the house is closer to a laboratory instrument, a device for registering and recording the events of the day. Use here is not so much a simple idea of practical function but an all-consuming sense of the building as a device, like a steam train or a spinning jenny.

Useless Architecture

Architecture is useless. Radically so.

The Swiss architect and theorist Bernard Tschumi once defined architecture as something beyond use. He was writing from a political point of view, defining architecture as something that can resist the domineering logic of society. His work explores architecture as an escape from use and the tyranny embodied in visions like Bentham's Panopticon. Pleasure, play and random acts of rebellion are more important than the prescribed uses of buildings. What happens to architecture when we misuse it?

The skateboarders who grind their way along the concrete landscape on London's South Bank are misusing architecture, and so, in effect, are the children playing football in the road or the squatters who turn an empty shop into their home. Architecture is misused all the time, in ways that are ad hoc and accidental or deliberate and provocative. Turning a spare bedroom into a workspace or an empty industrial unit into a nightclub are everyday forms of adaptation and reuse. In an era in which the demolition of buildings is seen as a waste of embodied carbon and energy, the reuse of buildings has become ever more important. How does this reflect on the relationship of architecture to use?

What happens when buildings outgrow their use? What happens when they effectively become useless, not in Tschumi's terms but in the literal sense? Sometimes they get demolished or are left to languish, but more often they get reused for other things. Churches become cafes and nurseries, offices become art galleries or lecture theatres and country houses become schools. Can buildings be designed for more than a single use? Are they defined by their use, or can they transcend single categories of use to become flexible, adaptable and useful in a generic, non-specific sense?

The idea of the loose-fit building persists as a counterpoint to extreme functionalism: architecture that is simple and adaptable enough to be used for many things. Industrial loft buildings with their simple, repetitive floor plate, lit by regular windows, are one example. The Georgian and Victorian terraced house is also cited as a flexible and easily adaptable type of architecture. Such terraces have been modified and adapted now for over two centuries, sometimes being converted into multiple dwellings and flats, into shops and offices and sometimes back into single-family houses. They have grown ground-floor and loft extensions, seen family life migrate from the first floor to the ground level and to large living and dining spaces that open out into the garden.

Is this a product of the innate adaptability of such buildings, or merely a result of their ubiquity? Certainly they were not designed to be adaptable. Some buildings are, though. The Centraal Beheer is an office building for an insurance company in built in Apeldoorn in 1972. On the face of it, an insurance company office doesn't sound like a particularly flexible building. Its use is specified, for a start. But beyond this, the design, by the Dutch architect Herman Hertzberger, aimed for a level of open-endedness and flexibility. The interior was designed to allow office workers to reconfigure the space and to maintain a level of autonomy and personal freedom. Unlike Bentham's Panopticon, the spatial design here deliberately allows people to hide from view, to carve out personal territory and alter the architecture around them. The structure of the building is both specific and loose, catering for the overall function while allowing for slippages around the edges.

Here is a building that is deliberately flexible and spatially messy. Contemporary photographs of it show the spaces occupied in loosely various ways. It is a middle-class factory that recognises the need for its employees' autonomy. This autonomy is expressed not in terms of wild individualism but – perhaps paradoxically – in a certain repetitive formality. Like the Palladian villa, a series of self-similar shapes proliferates across the site, each one ostensibly the same but able to allow for subtle reconfiguration and bespoke adaptability. Here is an idea that freedom lies not in wildly different individual expression but in a collective sense that everybody gets the same deal. While the overall use is prescribed, interpretation and modification of that is allowed within an egalitarian system. Each person is offered precisely the same amount of freedom.

Ordinary Use

We have looked at large spaces that allow lots of different uses and we have looked at buildings designed for very specific and literal uses. But use is something that permeates every scale of a building and contributes to our enjoyment and understanding of architecture. Use is there in the placement of a light socket and in the position of a window in a wall. It is inherent in what architects do when they design a building, but the thought behind it often goes unnoticed. It is only when buildings – and bits of buildings – *aren't* useful that we notice them.

Architect Margarete Schütte-Lihotzky designed what became known as the Frankfurt kitchen in 1926 as part of Ernst May's social housing project in New Frankfurt. Schütte-Lihotzky reinvented the kitchen as a separate functional room, distinct from other rooms but part of ordinary domestic life. It was designed ergonomically to make cooking easier and more straightforward, placing the main elements and appliances in relation to tasks. It was a time and motion study made manifest, owing as much to scientific management theory as to artistic currents of the time. It is both useful and beautiful, a coming together of practical necessity and elegance and a refined resolution of parts. Ten thousand Frankfurt kitchens were installed, and the design was undoubtedly an enormous success.

Kitchens are often as close as our houses get to being machines. They require a level of precision and detailed planning that makes them demanding to design and enraging when they don't work properly. Le Corbusier famously described the house as a machine for living in. This phrase has been much maligned since, mostly unfairly. We do want our houses to function as machines: we want them to keep us warm and our food cold, we want them to clean us and our clothes, allow us to work and sleep and cook and somehow do this while capturing our dreams. These activities are both generic and specific, inflected by circumstances and particular needs.

Sometimes architects take specific care to accommodate questions of use. The architects Herbert Tayler and David Green moved their practice from London to East Anglia in the period immediately following the Second World War. There they designed some 700 homes for villages in rural Norfolk, specialising in cheap and affordable modern houses that were superior to anything else being built at the time. This superiority was down to a careful analysis of need and the subtle accommodation of use.

Many of the houses that Tayler and Green designed were for agricultural workers, a fact that inflected their planning in intriguing and revealing ways. Tayler and Green developed their houses to reflect the lifestyle of their occupants. Dealing with the issue of workers coming home dirty from a day in the fields, they developed a plan with a wide, semi-external hallway that allowed for the removal of grubby clothes before entering the house proper. This hall also led directly to the garden, allowing equipment and machinery to be taken back and forth too. The kitchen overlooked this space, which led into a smaller, internal hall. It was a small but important gesture, one where the specifics of use helped to evolve a new kind of housing.

There is something pleasurable in this careful delineation of uses and the way that it is accommodated across the house. Looking at the plans of Tayler and Green is a pleasure, too. They are not drawn to impress other architects. They are not obviously or especially beautiful as drawings, though they are technically well drawn and laid out. They are undemonstrative, like the houses themselves. One can read the generosity of the spaces, though: how they are sized and oriented to aid certain kinds of action and how they interlink and add up to more than the sum of their parts. The shallow but wide houses that result from the internal planning give a languid and unhurried quality to the elevations, which combine to form streets and open spaces.

A few years ago, I travelled to Norfolk to visit some of Tayler and Green's houses. They built a lot, and little clusters of them seem to pop up everywhere. Despite their ordinariness, the houses still stand out. Something of the care that goes into their use is evident throughout, because ultimately the usefulness of them lies not only in the internal planning and the placement of windows and doors

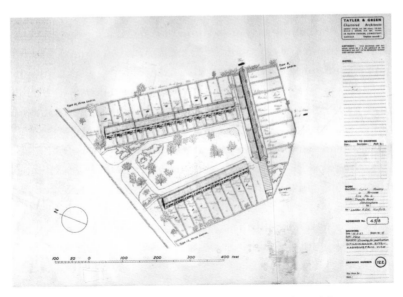

FIG. 31 Plan of Windmill Green, Norfolk, designed by Tayler and Green.

and rainwater goods but also in the placement of the houses within the landscape. They make spaces between them that are used for meeting and playing and simply enjoying the view. And they relate to the gentle, almost but not quite flat topography, so that they somehow complete the scene.

Windmill Green, built in Ditchingham in 1949 (fig. 31), is typical. The three long terraces of houses frame a triangular village green at the centre. We have already seen how the plans of these houses had evolved to allow generous and practical routes through the back gardens. Something similar happens on a wider scale, too. The ends of the terraces slide past each other in order to form discreetly private spaces to the rear where the bin stores and utility areas are located. They are easily accessible but largely hidden from view. There is a care and a careful appraisal of use at every level. Privacy, communality, aesthetic composition and attention to detail coalesce in small, intricate decisions that make up the whole.

The architects Alison and Peter Smithson tried to capture some of this sense of meaningful pragmatism in small decisions in their short essay 'In Praise of Cupboards'. The piece details the importance – and the pleasures – of good storage. And that's it. The Smithsons were radical architects, as radical in their way as Bernard Tschumi. And yet here they were talking about something as prosaic and humble as cupboards.

In Pevsner's terms, we have moved to an even more mundane world than the bicycle shed. But the Smithsons' essay is about removing certain things from our orbit in order to better concentrate on and enjoy the things that really matter. It is also about the small things, the minor details and concerns of architecture that, like a lot of issues around use, aren't particularly addressed by architectural theory but add enormously to the experience and the pleasures of good buildings.

Use as Art

So far in this chapter we have looked at use embodied in buildings for a single purpose (Bentham's Panopticon), at use accommodated in buildings that are generic and adaptable (Victorian terraces), and at use as small-scale and intimate problem-solving (Tayler and Green's Windmill Green). We have discussed use as something that directly shapes an entire building and use as something that is simply accommodated in subtle and unexpected ways.

When we use buildings, we expect them to work. We become irritated when they don't. But 'working' for buildings is not the same as 'working' for cars. Maybe when we are driving, we might accept minor faults, such as a flapping windscreen wiper or a broken cup holder. These don't alter the fundamental operational usefulness of the car, though they might be irritating or even dangerous. But a car that doesn't work is fundamentally useless in a way that architecture isn't. When buildings don't work well, when their usefulness is questionable, it can be in accumulative small ways or it can be through systemic breakdown. Often, too, it can go unregistered and unquestioned: an impractical layout, a damp patch on the wall.

Buildings don't work in the same way as machines. We might say a key difference is that they offer much more than machines, more than simply functionality. For example, we might say that they provide psychological shelter as well as physical shelter. But machines do that too. Numerous books and films have explored the psychological and emotional relationship people have with machines. Following Le Corbusier's dictum about 'houses as machines for living in', we could extend his comparison to other building types. A church is a machine for religious observance, for instance. And churches have ways to accommodate the various aspects of their services that inform the layout of the building. Church architecture follows the liturgical requirements of the specific branch of religion housed in it.

Another way of thinking about this might be to speak about ritual. We could talk about the house containing and giving spatial expression to the rituals of everyday life. These rituals contain conventions and rules (both unspoken and spoken) that influence how we live and organise ourselves. These rituals would include cooking, eating and sleeping, the way we gather to have dinner or compare notes on the day ahead over breakfast. These are the rhythms and routines of everyday life, and houses cater for them while also being a product of how they have evolved in specific cultures over time. In my house, for instance, we have a room in which we watch TV. The room is set up partially to do this, and my wife and children have their favourite spots to sit and their specific way of interacting while we watch. It is just a room, but it is organised around a use – watching TV – and that use is inflected by the specific rituals we have developed as a family.

Institutional buildings have their own rituals, rules and expectations too, sometimes explicit and sometimes buried below the water line. Sometimes these also explicitly shape and give expression to the building. To explore this relationship let's look at two very different buildings, one large, complex and institutional and the other small, relatively ordinary and dedicated to little more than having a good time.

The first is the Royal College of Physicians, a modernist building for a conservative client designed by Sir Denys Lasdun and completed in 1960. Like Lasdun's National Theatre on London's South Bank, the Royal College of Physicians is uncompromisingly modern and Brutalist in spirit. Lasdun was an architect with a taste for big, bold forms and for a certain kind of sculptural bravado. The National Theatre with its board-marked concrete and abstract shapes tends to divide opinion, but the Royal College of Physicians lives a quieter life on the edge of Regent's Park, shaded by trees and aligning – at least tonally – with the white stucco buildings of John Nash.

While it is abstract on the outside, the interior of the building is closely modelled on the rituals and symbolic activities of the college. Most memorably it contains a large, twisting staircase that takes you up to the formal and ceremonial hall at the top of the building. The stair is the route, and it forms the symbolic centrepiece of the interior. Membership of the Royal College of Physicians is via an entrance exam (among other things) culminating in an interview held in a formal room on the ground floor of the building. The interview room has two doors. If you pass the interview, you can leave the room via the door that takes you into the heart of the building. If you fail the interview, you return via the door you came in by. In a very real and physical sense the building acts as the spatial manifestation of the college, guarding entry against the uninitiated and framing the symbolic activities of the initiated.

Despite its modernity in stylistic terms, Lasdun's Royal College of Physicians is a very establishment building, one that reinforces the rites, rituals and rules of an age-old institution. It frames these rituals in elegant and sophisticated terms, and it makes a spatial virtue out of exclusive privilege. It is undoubtedly a great piece of architecture, one as conservative in some senses as the gentlemen's clubs of Pall Mall. It is a building framed internally by use in the most thoroughgoing way.

By way of contrast, we will move from Lasdun's large complex building in London to a small interior in Vienna. The American Bar was designed by Adolf Loos in 1908 and, remarkably, it is still there (fig. 32). Restaurants and bars don't usually last. By their nature they are transitory and subject to changes in taste and fashion. But Loos's bar has proved an insistent monument to the pleasures of drinking for over a hundred years.

We have already met Loos when discussing the subtle and psychologically complex houses he designed, mostly in Vienna. His American Bar contains similar ideas but on a smaller and even more intense scale. The bar announces itself to the street with a large mosaic sign depicting the US flag. At night, light shines through the small fragments of glass. Entering from the street, one passes through a strange, mirrored alcove below the sign. It is a deliberately disorienting moment, as if one is stepping out of one world and into another. Which is Loos's point. Inside the American Bar, it could be any time of day or night.

FIG. 32 American Bar, Vienna, designed by Adolf Loos.

The tiny interior is lined with richly reflective materials – marble, lacquered wood and brass. Light glints off the array of bottles behind the bar. The ceiling is coffered – that is, divided into a grid of recessed panels. Where the coffers meet the walls, Loos has installed mirrors so that the grid of panels appears to extend way beyond the limits of the actual space. It is a neat trick, one that increases the sense that the American Bar exists outside of both normal time and space. It is a place where a strong cocktail is always the right answer. Along the leading edge of the bar surface Loos has placed a thick, circular leather-clad tube to lean on. It is a useful object, but it is a joke, too. A man walks into a bar. At least in this case, it is a padded one.

This is a space as complex in its way as the Royal College of Physicians. Like Lasdun's building, it is shaped carefully around the rituals of its users. It can be crowded and lively or quiet and peaceful. With its disorienting reflections and surfaces, it is a space to lose oneself in. It is a supremely useful space but one dedicated to the luxury of wasting time.

The Architecture of Life

The evolution of buildings and their uses can be accidental and can happen over time. But it can also be planned. To conclude this chapter on use, I would like to return to an architect I mentioned right at the start. B.V. Doshi's career was long and illustrious. He began as something of a disciple of Le Corbusier and was awarded the Pritzker Prize – architecture's most important accolade – towards the end of his life in 2018. Most of his work is in India and it covers a vast range of building types and uses. Here we will consider just one of his projects, the Aranya housing scheme in Indore, begun in 1989 (fig. 33).

We have thought about use in terms of the careful and considered design of a building for a specific function. And we have

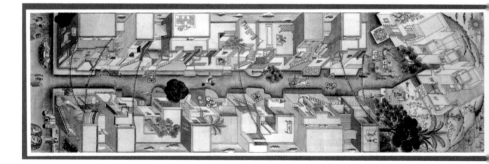

FIG. 33 Overview drawings of Aranya housing, Indore, designed by B.V. Doshi.

thought about use as something more transitory, something that occupies buildings regardless of what they were designed for. We have considered use as something large, important and fundamental to a building and as something, small, focused and specific, like a cupboard or a door handle. But what happens if we think of use not as a building exactly, but as a process, something neither designed specifically nor made to fit – something that is made meaningful only by its users? Aranya is an example of an architecture that is formed through use. It is a development for up to 80,000 people on an area of 85 hectares. Doshi's scheme for Aranya is really a framework for development by individuals. Plots are defined, services are provided and a foundation slab is built. Following this, individuals develop their houses in various ways using both stock parts and their own materials. Principles around density, traffic, public and private space are laid down, but much of the rest is left open.

Doshi's drawings for Aranya are extraordinary in themselves. There are many, describing everything from site arrangements to the multiple configurations of individual homes. But the most striking are those that depict an occupied street filled with houses and life. Architectural drawings tend to focus on architecture, unsurprisingly, rather than the life that architecture houses. Doshi's drawings here focus on use rather than building. Bicycles, plants, people, animals, taxis and mopeds fill the rooms and streets. Laundry flaps from the lines between houses. People lie on corners of grass or talk in courtyards. Somebody is selling fruit; someone else is buying a bunch of balloons. Two people appear to be praying.

The architecture of Aranya is a framework for things to happen. And use is defined not as 'house' or 'housing' but as multiple activities, *uses* in the widest and loosest sense. Use here is vital, neither central to an idea of the architecture nor peripheral and secondary. Instead, it is everywhere, permeating the spaces in ways that could never be fully captured by even the most wide-ranging architectural brief. Architects tend to see use as something singular and specific: library, school, house, factory, farm. But here use is really something else, something more general, something more like life.

Perhaps here we have arrived at an explanation of how we can really and most profoundly enjoy architecture. It is both background and foreground, something that we shape but which also shapes us. Something useful that also brings profound pleasure. Something massive that is also about space. Something structural that contains pattern, colour and ornament. Something material that is also about the intangible and fleeting pleasures of life. It is not quite true to say that architecture is at its most profound when it becomes the background to everything else. It is foreground, too. It is a source of intense enjoyment that allows us to enjoy so much else as well.

FURTHER READING

Bawa, Geoffrey, *The Complete Works* (London and New York: Thames and Hudson, 2002)

Betsky, Aaron, *The Complete Zaha Hadid* (London: Thames and Hudson, 2013; rev. edn, 2017)

Brittain-Catlin, Timothy, *The Edwardians and Their Houses: The New Life of Old England* (London: Lund Humphries, 2020)

The Buildings of England (Pevsner Architectural Guides) (1951–74, and since revised)

Colomina, Beatriz, *Privacy and Publicity* (Cambridge, MA: MIT Press, 1994)

Le Corbusier, *Towards a New Architecture* (1923; multiple editions available in English)

Curtis, William, *Denys Lasdun: Architecture, City, Landscape* (London: Phaidon, 1994)

Curtis, William, and Balkrishna Doshi, *Balkrishna Doshi: An Architecture for India* (New York: Rizzoli, 1988)

Evans, Robin, *Translations from Drawing to Building and Other Essays* (London: Architectural Association, 2021)

Fletcher, Sir Banister, *Global History of Architecture* (1896; 21st edition, London: Bloomsbury, 2019)

Frampton, Kenneth, *Modern Architecture: A Critical History* (1980; 5th edition, London: Thames and Hudson, 2020)

Frank, Susan, and Peter Eisenman, *Peter Eisenman's House VI: The Client's Response* (New York: Whitney Library of Design, 1994)

Graham, Dan, *Rock My Religion: Writings and Projects 1965–1990* (Cambridge, MA: MIT Press, 1994)

Harwood, Elain, and Alan Powers, *Tayler and Green Architects: The Spirit of Place in Modern Housing* (London: Prince of Wales's Institute of Architecture, 1998)

Hitchmough, Wendy, *C.F.A. Voysey* (London: Phaidon, 1997)

Jencks, Charles, *Modern Movements in Architecture* (Harmondsworth: Penguin, 1983)

Krohn, Carsten, *Mies van der Rohe: The Built Work* (Basel: Birkhäuser, 2014)

Krucker, Bruno, and Stephen Bates, *The Country Houses of Palladio, Veneto* (Munich: Studio Krucker Bates, 2022)

Lawrence, Amanda, *James Stirling: Revisionary Modernist* (New Haven and London: Yale University Press, 2013)

Loos, Adolf, *Spoken into the Void: Collected Essays*, trans. J.O. Newman and J.H. Smith (Cambridge, MA: MIT Press, 1982)

Mawer, Simon, *The Glass Room* (London: Little, Brown, 2009)

Musson, Jeremy, *Robert Adam: Country House Design, Decoration and the Art of Elegance* (New York: Rizzoli, 2017)

Rossi, Aldo, *The Architecture of the City*, trans. Diane Ghirardo and Joan Ockman (Cambridge, MA: MIT Press, 1982)

Rowe, Colin, and Fred Koetter, *Collage City* (Cambridge, MA: MIT Press, 1978)

Shinohara, Kazuo, *Casas / Houses* (Barcelona: Gustavo Gili, 2011)

Smithson, Alison and Peter, *From the House of the Future to a House of Today* (Rotterdam: 010 Publishers, 2004)

Sontag, Susan, *Against Interpretation* (1966; multiple editions available)

Stamp, Gavin, *Edwin Lutyens: Country Houses* (New York: Monacelli Press, 2009)

Summerson, Sir John, *The Classical Language of Architecture* (London: Thames and Hudson, 1980)

———— *Heavenly Mansions, and Other Essays on Architecture* (London: Cresset Press, 1949)

Tschumi, Bernard, *Questions of Space* (London: AA Publications, 1995)

Venturi, Robert, *Complexity and Contradiction in Architecture* (New York: Museum of Modern Art, 1966)

Watari, Etsuko (ed.), *Lina Bo Bardi* (Tokyo: Toto, 2017)

ACKNOWLEDGEMENTS

This book has been a long time in the making. I have practised, enjoyed and occasionally been exasperated by architecture for over three decades now. During that time many people, books and buildings have influenced my thinking and helped open my eyes to the joys of architecture.

My undergraduate tutor, Robin Evans, introduced me to architectural history in a way that still shapes how I look at buildings today. For the best part of twenty years my colleagues at FAT, Sean Griffiths and Sam Jacob, provided a source of daily inspiration. The work of Denise Scott Brown and Robert Venturi has been hugely important, not least in demonstrating the creative relationship between words and buildings. And Grayson Perry made the job of being an architect more enjoyable than I had previously thought possible.

Various people have commissioned me to write for them over the years, including Fatema Ahmed, Isabel Allen, Amanda Baillieu, Johanna Dale, Hayley Dixon, Mark Fisher, Merlin Fulcher, Phin Harper, Owen Hatherley, Owen Hopkins, Kieran Long, Justin McGuirk, Hugh Pearman, Eleanor Young and Will Wiles, and I am grateful to them all. Will Wiles went one step further and – together with Hazel Tsoi-Wiles – commissioned me to design their house. I hope they enjoy living in it as much as I enjoyed designing it.

For ideas, conversations and inspiration along the way I would like to thank Marie Bek-Mortensen, Rafe Bertram, Timothy Brittain-Catlin, Gillian Darley, Christian Ducker, Travis Elborough, Jon Goodbun, Edwin Heathcote, Joanna Jones, Verity-Jane Keefe,

David Knight, David Kohn, Di Mainstone, Cristina Monteiro, Rowan Moore, Patrick O'Keeffe, Ruth Lang, Mark Robinson, Karen Skurlock, Catherine Slessor, Daniel Stilwell and Cordula Weisser.

I would also like to thank my editor, Sophie Neve, who commissioned this book for Yale University Press in the first place and who guided its development with such care, and Susannah Stone, who patiently sourced all the images, even the ones added at the last minute.

Lastly, and most importantly, I would like to thank my wife Jenny, for encouraging me to write this book and for so much else.